Company Secretary's Briefing

Third Edition

GW00504491

Revised reprint 1995
Second edition 1997
Third edition 2000

ISBN 1 86089 669 3

Gee Publishing Ltd.
100 Avenue Road
Swiss Cottage
London NW3 3PG

Printed in Great Britain by
Unwin Brothers Ltd, The Gresham Press, Old Woking, Surrey

Introduction

For the company administrator the Companies Act 1985 brought clarification of the law affecting companies as it consolidated into one Act the legislation contained in the Companies Act 1948 as amended by the Companies Acts of 1967, 1976, 1980 and 1981. This situation, which made it easier to establish the current legislation, was short-lived as the Companies Act 1985 was itself amended by the The Insolvency Act 1986, The Financial Services Act 1986 and The Directors' Disqualification Act 1986. The position was further complicated by the Companies Act 1989 which severely altered and amended the 1985 Act.

One of the complications of the 1989 Act is that it introduces sections into the 1985 Act, which are to be known as sections of the 1985 Act except that they do not physically appear in that Act but in the 1989 Act. The 1989 Act also amends various sections of the 1985 Act and replaces sections 221 to 262 (accounts and audit) by new sections using the same section numbers. Great care has to be taken therefore to ensure that when a reference is made to the Companies Act 1985 it is clear whether it is the original enactment or an amendment in the 1989 Act that reflects the current law.

Further amendments, additions and deletions to the 1985 Act have been made by sundry Statutory Instruments issued since the 1989 Act received the Royal Assent, and not all of these Statutory Instruments have been issued under the Companies Act 1989, but sometimes under other Acts of Parliament.

In this book a reference to a section number or a schedule number refers to the 1985 Act unless stated otherwise. Where that section or schedule is introduced into the 1985 Act by the 1989 Act there is shown in brackets the section number in the Companies Act 1989 (CA 1989) where it appears for ease of reference. In other cases, where appropriate, the full title of the instrument bringing in the amendment to the law is shown.

This period of great change in company legislation has been accompanied by the change in Companies House status so that it is now an Executive Agency. This has brought a greater awareness of the requirements of users of the information stored by Companies House and a greatly enhanced effort to secure compliance by companies with their filing requirements. All company administrators must be aware of their obligations and mindful of the penalties for non-compliance which in several areas are being applied with vigour.

3

This volume has been written especially with the smaller company in mind to help them cope with the myriad of rules which exist and to enable them to avoid the penalties waiting to catch the unwary.

Corporate governance has also come under examination recently with the publication of various committee reports. The recommendations of these committees have been joined together in the Combined Code which now forms part of the stock exchange listing rules. We have also had the Turnbull Report giving guidance on how the Combined Code should be implemented. These reports specifically targeted public companies but many of the underlying principles apply equally to private companies. There is a need, therefore, for all companies to ensure that they are not only complying with the letter of the law but also complying with the spirit of the law.

The Government has initiated a very wide-ranging review of company law upon which there is to be wide consultation involving the business community. The results of this review will be the subject of a new Companies Act but this is not scheduled to be introduced during the life of the current Parliament.

Contents

7 Directors

13

22 Striking off and dissolution

Glossary

Maintenance of Registers

■ CHAPTER ONE ■

Contents

■ KEY QUESTIONS ■

Who can inspect the statutory books and what copies must be provided?

Does the company have to provide other facilities for persons inspecting the records?

What fees may be charged for inspection and the provision of copies?

What information has to be kept about Directors and the Secretary and does it have to be returned to Companies House?

What information has to be kept on the Register of Members?

Does the company have to keep a Register of Debenture Holders?

What information has to be kept concerning Directors' interests in the shares and debentures of the company?

Does the company have to keep available for inspection details of Directors' share options?

Where does the company record details of any substantial holdings of the company's securities notified to it?

Who can inspect copies of instruments creating a charge which have been registered at Companies House?

What information has to be kept in the Register of Charges?

1:1 Introduction

The company must keep all the statutory books which are recorded below. In practice this means that they are kept by the Company Secretary, or, that the holder of that office accepts responsibility for them and ensures that they are kept properly including making sure that entries are made within the time limits set down in the Act.

1:2 Rights of inspection

The Registers are open to inspection to the extent mentioned against each Register below. The general rules concerning inspection are contained in The Companies (Inspection and Copying of Registers, Indices and Documents) Regulations 1991 (SI 1991 No.1998) and state that where inspection is allowed the records must be available for at least two hours between 9.00am and 5.00pm every working day, and the company does not have to supply any facilities other than those required to facilitate inspection. A company need not comply with a request to group information in its Register of Members or its Register of Debenture Holders or supply copies from those Registers grouped by geographical location, nationality, size of holding, whether natural persons or corporations, or gender.

1:3 Fees chargeable

The company may make a charge for inspecting its registers or supplying extracts there from. The fees sanctioned by the Act are:

Inspection: • **£2.50 per hour or part thereof for non–members but free for members.**

Extracts: • **£2.50 for the first 100 entries or part thereof.**

• **£20.00 for the next 1,000 entries or part thereof.**

• **£15.00 per 1,000 entries or part thereof subsequently.**

The permitted charge for supplying copies of trust deeds and minutes remains at ten pence per 100 words or part thereof.

1:4 Register of Directors and Secretary (ss.288, 289 and 290)

This Register shall contain for Directors the following information:

In the case of an individual:

- **present name. Full christian or fore names are required, initials will not suffice;**
- **former name** — *see* **below;**
- **usual residential address. Company's Registered Office is not acceptable unless it is the private residence of that Director;**
- **nationality;**
- **business occupation;**
- **other Directorships. Dormant companies and other companies within a group are not required. Past Directorships held within the last five years must be included;**
- **date of birth.**

In the case of a corporation:

- **Corporate or Scottish Firm name;**
- **Registered or Principal Office.**

The Register shall contain for the Secretary the following information.

In the case of an individual:

- **present name — full christian or fore names are required;**
- **former name** — *see* **below;**
- **usual residential address.**

In the case of a Partnership acting as Joint Secretaries:

- **the Firm name;**
- **principal address.**

A former name does not include:

(a) a name by which a lady was known prior to marriage;

(b) a name not used since the attainment of 18 years of age;

(c)   a name not used for over 20 years;

(d)   a name by which a peer was known prior to his/her accession to the peerage.

Any addition, deletion or alteration to the information contained in the Register must be notified to Companies House on the appropriate form stating the date the change took place and be notified to them within 14 days of that date.

The appropriate forms are:

(a)   Form 288a for the appointment of a new Director or Secretary;

(b)   Form 288b for the resignation or removal of a Director or Secretary;

(c)   Form 288c for the change in any of the particulars of a Director or Secretary.

Where the Form 288a records the appointment of a Director or Secretary it must be signed by the person accepting the appointment in addition to being signed on behalf of the company.

The Register is open to inspection by both members and non–members and must be kept at the Registered Office. There is no requirement to provide copies of this Register.

1:5   Register of Members (s.352 *et seq.*)

The Register shall contain the following information:

(a)   name and address of all members;

(b)   date when the member was first registered;

(c)   date when the member ceased membership for past shareholders;

(d)   if shares have been issued, the number of shares held with share numbers, if applicable, and the amount paid up on each share, all split between the various classes of shares;

(e)   if shares have been converted into stock and notice of the conversion has been given to the Registrar then the amount of stock held;

(f)   details of past members for the last 20 years.

If the company becomes a Single Member Company then by s.352A [The Companies (Single Member Private Limited Companies) Regulations 1992 (SI 1992 No.1699)] there must be recorded in the Register of Members:

(a)   the name and address of the sole member;

(b)   a statement that the company has only one member;

(c)   the date that the change took place.

Similarly, where a Single Member Company acquires additional members there must be entered in the Register of Members:

(a)   the name and address of the person who was the sole member;

(b)   a statement that the company is no longer a Single Member Company;

(c)   the date that the change took place.

Although this information is readily available from an examination of the Register it is suggested that the Act would seem to require a separate set of statements to satisfy s.352A.

The Register must be kept at the Registered Office unless notice has been given to the Registrar on Form 353 that it is being kept elsewhere. If the company keeps its Register on a computer, the address where those records may be inspected, if not at the Registered Office, must be notified to Companies House on Form 353a. A company registered in England and Wales must keep its Register within England and Wales and similarly a company registered in Scotland must keep its Register within Scotland. If the records are kept on a computer the address where the records may be inspected must be within the country of registration.

If there are more than 50 members, unless the Register is self-indexing, an index must be kept, which must be amended within 14 days of the Register being altered.

No notice of any trust may be entered on the Register of any company registered in England and Wales (s.360). This means that if a third party acquires an interest in shares, as for example when a Bank takes a charge over the shares as security for an overdraft, no notice of that interest may be entered on the Register and the company need only deal with the registered holder as the person entitled to deal with those shares. These regulations do not apply to companies registered in Scotland where notices served on the company have to be recorded on the Share Register.

26

The Register is open to inspection to both members and non–members and copies of the Register may be required and must be supplied within ten days.

If information additional to that required by these regulations, for example members' bank details for the payment of dividends, is held on the Register then that information does not have to be made available for inspection, and it is suggested should not be made available for inspection as it was not given to the company for inspection purposes. Under current data protection legislation, if the Register is kept on computer and contains only that information required by statute, it does not come within the provisions for registration, but will need to be registered if additional information is held.

1:6   Register of Debenture Holders (ss.190 and 191)

There is no requirement for a company to keep a Register of Debenture Holders and where one is kept it is not laid down what information must be contained in that Register. Where a company issues a series of debentures it will of necessity need to keep this Register to keep a record of the holders of those debentures to whom it must pay interest at the appropriate intervals. The security for the debenture holders will be a charge upon certain assets of the company held by a trustee on their behalf and that charge must also be recorded in the Register of Charges (*see* **1:9**). The Act does stipulate that if a Register is kept for a company registered in England and Wales it must be kept in England and Wales and similarly for a company registered in Scotland it must be kept in Scotland. If a Register of overseas Debenture Holders is kept outside of Great Britain any duplicate of that Register kept within Great Britain must be kept with the main Register. If the Register and any duplicate are kept other than at the Registered Office notification must be given to Companies House on Form 190.

The Register is open to inspection to both members and debenture holders free of charge and to non–members when the fees set out above (*see* **1:3**) may be levied. Copies of the Register may be requested. Debenture holders may also request copies of any trust deed securing an issue of debentures.

If Debenture Holders' bank details for the payment of interest are held on this Register the comments at the end of **section 1:5** apply equally in this case.

1:7   Register of Directors' Interests (s.325)

Directors have an obligation to notify any company of which they are a Director of their interests in the company and other companies within the Group. The company must record all of this information in its Register of Directors' Interests. It should be noted that 'interests' include not only holdings of shares and debentures but rights or options to subscribe for shares or debentures.

Upon appointment, a Director must notify the company in writing within five days of any interest in shares or debentures of the company, a subsidiary company, its holding company or a fellow subsidiary of the holding company. These regulations also apply to a Shadow Director and the notification must include not only the interests of the Director but those of his/her spouse and any dependent children.

A Director who holds shares as a bare trustee or custodian trustee or under Scottish law as a simple trustee does not come within the scope of these regulations.

Under the Companies (Disclosure of Directors' Interests) (Exceptions) Regulations 1985 (SI 1985 No. 802) a person who is a Director of the holding company and of a subsidiary company need not notify his/her interests to the subsidiary company provided they are recorded by the holding company. A Director need not also notify any interests in companies incorporated overseas.

There is a continuing obligation upon a Director to notify the company in writing within five days of the happening of any of the events set out below:

(a)   becoming or ceasing to be interested in any shares or debentures of the company;

(b)   entering a contract to sell the company's shares or debentures;

(c)   assignment of a right to subscribe for shares in his/her own company;

(d)   grant to him/her of a right to subscribe for shares, the exercise of that right or assignment of that right in a connected company.

Notification must be in writing within five days of the occurrence of the event giving rise to the notification and must state the number and class of shares or the amount of debentures involved. The notification must contain a statement that it is in satisfaction of the Director's obligations under s.325.

Where a Director is granted a right to subscribe for shares, that is an option to subscribe for shares at some future date at a fixed price or at a price calculated from a formula set down in the grant, these rights must be declared in his/her record of interests.

Where the rights are in the company of which the person is a Director then it is the company's obligation to ensure that they are recorded when they are granted or are exercised, but it is the Director's obligation to notify the company if they are assigned to a third party.

Where the rights are in an associated company then it is for the Director to notify the company when they are granted, exercised or assigned.

Where a right to subscribe for shares is granted there must also be shown in the Register:

(a)   date that the right was granted;

(b)   period during which the right is exercisable;

(c)   consideration for the grant of the right including nil if that be the case;

(d)   description of the shares and debentures involved.

The company must record all of this information in its Register and entries should be made within three days of notification. An index shall be kept which should be brought up to date within 14 days of an entry being made in the Register.

The Register should be kept at the company's Registered Office but may be kept with the Register of Members if that is kept elsewhere. If the Register is not kept at the Registered Office notification of its location must be given to the Registrar on Form 325. The Register is open to inspection by both members and non–members and also has to be available for inspection at the Annual General Meeting. Copies of all or part of the Register may be requested and must be supplied within ten days.

1:8 Register of Substantial Holdings (s.211 (s.134, CA 1989))

Any person who on his/her own or in conjunction with others acquires an interest of three per cent or more in the equity of a public company must notify the company in writing within two days of acquiring that interest. The notification to the company is the percentage holding rounded down to the nearest whole number and any change in the holding which alters that whole number including dropping below the three per cent threshold must be similarly notified.

Under the Disclosure of Interests in Shares (Amendment) Regulations 1993 (SI 1993 No. 1819) a public company which has a Stock Exchange listing must also be advised where a person has an interest in ten per cent or more of the equity of the company when aggregating both material and non-material holdings. Material holdings are where the registered holder has a beneficial interest in the shares. Non-material holdings are where the registered holder has control over the shares but no beneficial interest as, for example, in the case of a unit trust manager, investment trust manager or share club manager.

Every public company must keep a register of the information notified to it, entries being made in chronological order within three days of notification. An index should be kept which should be updated within ten days of the Register being altered.

The Register must be kept at the same location as the Register of Directors' Shareholdings so notification to the Registrar is NOT required if this is not at the Registered Office.

The Register is open to inspection to both members and non–members free of charge and copies may be requested which must be supplied within ten days for which the fees set out above (*see* **1:3**) may be charged.

If the company ceases to be a public company the Register must be retained for six years.

1:9 Register of Charges (s.407 and s.422)

Every company must keep at its Registered Office a Register to record the details of all charges required to be registered with Companies House. There shall be kept with the Register copies of the instruments creating the charge, or in the case of a series of debentures one of the series. The Register shall contain brief details of the property charged, the amount of the charge and the beneficiaries of the charge.

The Register and the copy instruments are open to inspection to both members and creditors free of charge. Currently, the Register only is open to inspection by non-members and a fee not exceeding five pence may be charged. Under the existing legislation there is no provision for obtaining copies of the Register or the copy instruments. The 1989 Act contains provisions for revision of the Register of Charges but they are now most unlikely to be enacted in that form. Alternative proposals are now under consideration.

The requirements of Companies House for the registration of a charge or notification of its subsequent release are set out in Chapter 20.

■ CHECK LIST ■

Are there arrangements in place to cope with
requests to inspect the Registers and to
provide copies? ☐

Are details of Directors and Secretary up-to-date
especially with regard to residential address and
other Directorships? ☐

Is the Register of Members up-to-date? ☐

If the company is a single member company have
details been recorded in the Register of Members? ☐

Does the company have a Register of Debenture
Holders and is it up-to-date? ☐

Have the Directors notified all their interests for
inclusion in the Register of Directors Interests
including those of their spouse and any
dependent children and any rights to subscribe
granted to them? ☐

Have any substantial holdings been notified to the
company and have they been recorded? ☐

Is the Register of Charges up-to-date and have all
satisfied charges been removed from the record? ☐

Other statutory requirements and Records

■ CHAPTER TWO ■

Contents

■ KEY QUESTIONS ■

Does the company have to have a seal?

How can the company execute a deed without a seal?

Does usage of the Seal have to be recorded?

Does the company have to keep minutes of all meetings?

Can members inspect the minutes?

Does the company have to keep Directors' service contracts available for inspection?

Who can inspect the Directors' service contracts?

Do the members have to approve Directors' service contracts?

Outside which premises must a company display its name?

Where else must a company display its name?

What are the penalties for a person who issues a cheque not signed for and on behalf of the company?

What information must be shown on the company's letterheading?

2:1 The Company Seal

Up until the introduction of the relevant sections of the Companies Act 1989 a company entered into a Deed by affixing to the document its common seal and that sealing being attested in accordance with the company's Articles, usually by the signatures of a Director and the Secretary or two Directors.

Section 36A (s.130, CA 1989) provides that a company need not have a seal but where a document is signed by a Director and the Secretary or by two Directors and it is made clear that it is to have effect as if it was sealed, then it will be considered as having been executed as if it had been sealed.

It must, however, be made clear that the document was executed with the intention of being regarded as having been sealed. It is suggested, therefore, that the words set out below or something similar are written immediately above the signatures:

'Executed as a Deed on behalf of XYZ Ltd.'

If the powers are given in the Articles, the Directors can delegate the use of the Seal to other officers in the company as often happens where the Registrar seals share certificates. Under the provisions of s.36A these powers to dispense with the Seal cannot be delegated and any document executed under hand but which is to be regarded as sealed must contain the signatures of a Director and the Secretary or two Directors.

If a company does have a subsidiary seal for use by the Registrar or in an overseas country it will only be valid so long as the company does retain its common seal.

Where the Articles specify that a particular type of document must be executed under seal then the company will be bound by its Articles and not be able to take advantage of these new provisions.

Section 36B (s.130, CA 1989) states that where a company registered in Scotland executes a Deed in accordance with s.36A the signatures must be witnessed, but that need for witnessing has now been set aside by the Law Reform (Miscellaneous Provisions) (Scotland) Act 1990. Further change to the law affecting Scottish companies and their powers to execute deeds was brought about by Paragraph 51, Schedule 4 of the Requirements of Writing (Scotland) Act 1995. Under that legislation a company registered in Scotland may execute a deed without the use of its seal by the signatures of a Director and the Company Secretary or of two

Directors or of two authorised persons. It is emphasised that the signatures must be one of those specified combinations. The legislation further provides that execution may also be effected by the signature by one of those named persons with that signature being witnessed.

Where a company does have a seal then the company name must be engraved on it in legible characters (s.350).

A company may have a subsidiary seal for use overseas and such a seal must be a copy of the common seal with the addition of the name of the country or countries where it may be used (s.39). Similarly, a company may have a subsidiary seal for use on securities and this must be a copy of the common seal with the addition of the word 'securities' (s.40).

The Seal must be kept in a place of safety and secure from unauthorised use. Every usage shall be in accordance with the company's Articles and minuted or recorded in a Seal Register which should be brought before each Board Meeting for ratification.

2:2   Minutes of meetings

It is a statutory requirement (s.382) for minutes to be kept of all general meetings (that is meetings of members) of the company and of all meetings of Directors otherwise known as board meetings. Minutes of meetings of Directors should be kept separately from those of general meetings as members are entitled to inspect minutes of general meetings but have no right of access to Board minutes. Members may request copies of general meeting minutes which must be supplied within seven days.

Minutes of Directors' meetings are confidential to the Directors although the Auditors have a right of inspection as do certain government officials.

Minutes are a record of decisions taken at a meeting, they are not a verbatim record of the proceedings of a meeting. General meetings are called to consider specific resolutions and to pass or reject those resolutions. The notice of the meeting will set out the business of the meeting including the wording of resolutions to be proposed other than for the routine business of the Annual General Meeting and the minutes will similarly record the decisions taken including the full wording of those resolutions. There is unlikely to be much, if any, background information to the results of the meeting. Board meetings are called to discuss matters of interest and only infrequently will have specific resolutions before them. Most decisions will be by concensus and the minutes will record those decisions. By the nature of board meetings their minutes are much more likely to contain some background information to the decisions reached but they will still not be a verbatim record of the proceedings.

By s.382B where the sole member of a Single Member Company takes a decision which may have been taken by a company in general meeting and has effect as if agreed by a company in general meeting, then, unless it was agreed as a written resolution, it must be evidenced in writing by the member. Failure to do so will not invalidate the decision but will lay the member open to penalties.

2:3 Directors' service contracts

By s.318 a company must keep a copy of every service contract with the company or a subsidiary company for a Director or Shadow Director or, where the contract is not in writing, a written memorandum of its contents. The contracts which come within the scope of this regulation are those with a year or more unexpired unless they may be terminated within one year without the payment of compensation.

The copies shall be kept together and may be kept at the Registered Office, with the Register of Members if that is kept elsewhere or at the company's principal place of business provided that is within the country of Registration. If they are not kept at the Registered Office notification must be given to the Registrar on Form 318. The contracts are open to inspection by members only free of charge.

The Act does not give a definition of what comprises a service contract but from the restriction on those which have to be kept by the company it is obviously a contract which gives a guarantee of continuity of employment or alternatively financial compensation for a period in excess of that normally offered to employees. It would also be something far more substantial than a contract of employment which has to be given to all employees. Unless otherwise stated a Director is regarded as an office holder rather than an employee. Whilst it may be felt desirable to document in the service contract that Directors, especially full time executive Directors, are employees there have been a number of recent court cases where the written statement has been ignored and on the facts of the case the court has ruled that the Director was an office holder.

Any service contract for a Director for a period in excess of five years is subject to agreement by the company in general meeting by ordinary resolution. Contracts for a period of five years or less may be agreed by the Directors themselves.

Where a meeting is called to agree a contract which has a term in excess of five years a copy of the contract must be available for inspection by members of the company at the Registered Office for 15 days prior to the meeting and at the meeting itself.

2:4 Display of company name

By s.348 every company must display its name outside every office and business premises which it occupies in a conspicuous position and in letters easily legible. Care should be taken to ensure that in multi-use office premises it is easily ascertainable which parts of the premises are occupied by the company.

Where the Registered Office is in premises that are otherwise not used by the company, for example in the offices of professional advisors or the private residence of a Director, they are still regarded as business premises of the company and the company name must be displayed.

By s.349 a company must also state its name in:

(a)   all business letters of the company;

(b)   all its notices and other official publications;

(c)   all bills of exchange, promissory notes, endorsements, cheques and orders for money or goods purporting to be signed by or on behalf of the company;

(d)   all bills of parcels, invoices, receipts and letters of credit.

In both these sections, reference to the company name means the full name, spelt exactly as registered and including Public Limited Company or Limited or their accepted abbreviations. The company logo which does not include all of these particulars will not satisfy the legislation.

Section 349 also states that any person who issues a bill of exchange, promissory note, endorsement, cheque or order for money or goods which does not state the name of the company is liable to a fine and may also be personally liable if the amount due is not paid by the company. With regard to these documents the person signing must be seen to be signing for and on behalf of the company and the company name should appear immediately above the signature.

The danger of issuing a cheque not in accordance with the law is minimal now that cheques are generally pre–printed with the company name but care should be taken that the name is complete and properly spelt. Attention should also be given to standing orders and direct debits where they are generally completed on standard stationery of the supplier. It should be made clear that any signature on a standing order or direct debit is made for and on behalf of the company. Similarly, company order forms should be printed so that the issuer always signs for and on behalf of the company.

Section 351 states that all business letters and order forms of the company shall show:

(a)   the company's place of registration and the number with which it is registered;

(b)   the address of the Registered Office;

(c)   in the case of an investment company, the fact that it is such a company;

(d)   in the case of a company exempt from the need to use 'limited' as part of its name, the fact that it is a limited company.

Where the address shown at the head of business stationery is the Registered Office it would seem that this is sufficient to comply with the Act. It is suggested, however, that it is good practice to confirm that the address shown is that of the Registered Office.

Section 111 of the Companies Act 1989 inserts s.30C into the Charities Act 1960 and states that where a company is a charity and its name does not include the words 'charity' or 'charitable' it must state the fact that it is a charity wherever its name appears.

Thus all those items mentioned above under s.349 must show that a company is a charity if the name does not convey this fact. This includes promissory notes, cheques, etc. which must carry this statement that the company is a charity otherwise the issuer could be liable to a fine and personally liable on the cheque if it is not met. Probably the simplest way to indicate that a company is a charity is to state the charity number.

Although the Charities Act 1960 does not apply to Scotland, s.112(6) of the Companies Act 1989 extends similar provisions to companies registered in Scotland which are charities.

■ CHECK LIST ■

Is it clear whether contracts entered under hand
are to be regarded as having been sealed? ☐

Are Directors aware that contracts can be entered
under hand with the legal consequences as if
they had been sealed? ☐

Do the Articles specify the use of the Seal in
respect of any particular matters? ☐

Does the company have subsidiary Seals and are
they being used properly? ☐

Is the Company Seal correctly titled and does it
reflect any change of name? ☐

Are all uses of the Seal minuted or entered in a
Seal Register? ☐

Is the Seal secure from any unauthorised use? ☐

Are minutes kept of all Directors' and General
Meetings? ☐

Are Directors' minutes kept separately so that General
Meeting minutes can be made available for inspection? ☐

Does the company have a copy of all Directors'
service contracts? ☐

Is the company name displayed outside all
company premises? ☐

Is the name displayed on stationery and other
company documentation? ☐

Do persons signing cheques and orders sign for
and on behalf of the company? ☐

Is the full name displayed in all these places? ☐

Does company stationery show the address of the
Registered Office, where the company is
registered and the registered number? ☐

Secretarial aspects of Annual Accounts

■ CHAPTER THREE ■

Contents

■ KEY QUESTIONS ■

What books of account does the company have to keep?

Does the company have to notify Companies House where accounting records are kept?

Who has access to the books of account?

What returns does the company have to have from its overseas interests?

How long do accounting records have to be retained?

Can the Accounting Reference Date be changed?

What documents have to be included with the Accounts?

Who approves the Accounts and Directors' Report?

Who signs the Balance Sheet and the Directors' Report?

Who is entitled to copies of our Accounts?

What are the time limits for laying and filing Accounts?

Are there penalties if Accounts are filed late?

If the Accounts are found to be incorrect what happens?

Who can file abbreviated Accounts?

Who can issue summary financial statements?

How does the company dispense with laying Accounts before a general meeting?

Does a dormant company have to prepare Accounts?

Can the company dispense with an audit?

If the company had planned to dispense with an audit does eligibility still exist?

What information has to be included in the Directors' Report?

3:1 Statutory requirement to keep Accounts

The statutory basis for a company to keep accounts is provided by s.221 (s.2, CA 1989) which states that records shall be kept sufficient for the following purposes:

- **To disclose the financial position of the company.**

- **To enable a Profit and Loss Account and Balance Sheet to be prepared.**

- **To contain from day-to-day, records of all sums received and expended.**

- **To give details of assets and liabilities.**

- **If the company deals in goods**

  — **to show the stock held at the end of each year;**

  — **apart from retail sales, to show details of all goods sold and purchased.**

The Directors do also have a duty to manage the business to the best of their ability and this would undoubtedly encompass keeping not only these specific records but any others required to monitor the day-to-day financial progress of the company.

3:1.1 Where Records may be kept

The accounting records may be kept wherever the Directors think fit and the address at which they are kept does not have to be notified to the Registrar.

3:1.2 Directors' access to Records

The accounting records are open to inspection by the company's officers at all times (s.222(1) (s.2, CA 1989)). It is thought that the literal interpretation of this last directive could at times bring administrative difficulties to the company and it is therefore suggested that it should be translated as meaning that all officers are entitled to financial information and to have their requests met for answers to specific questions.

3:1.3   Overseas interests

If accounting records are kept overseas then returns must be made to Great Britain at least every six months to show the financial position with reasonable accuracy and to enable the Directors to prepare Accounts in accordance with the requirements of the Act.

3:1.4   Retention of Records

The accounting records which the company is obliged to keep by the provisions of the Companies Act must be retained for a period of three years for a private company and for a period of six years for a public company. These periods for retention of accounting records may, however, be insufficient for other legislation, for example Income Tax, Corporation Tax and Value Added Tax.

3:2   Accounting Reference Date

Every company must have an Accounting Reference Date and that date is of the company's own choosing. For a newly incorporated company the Accounting Reference Date will automatically be the last day of the month of incorporation unless the appropriate form is submitted to select an alternative date. Every company must make up its Accounts for its accounting reference period ending on its Accounting Reference Date or on a date not more than seven days either side of that day. The Accounts shall cover the period since the date to which the last Accounts were prepared. A company's first Accounts must not be for a period of less than six months nor for a period of more than 18 months.

3:2.1   Change of Accounting Reference Date

A company may change its Accounting Reference Date by filing with the Registrar Form 225. This form may be used to alter the Accounting Reference Date of the current accounting reference period or of the previous accounting reference period provided the latest date for filing accounts for that period has not passed.

Normally, a company is not allowed to extend its accounting reference period more than once in five years unless it is to bring it into line with other group companies (see below) or where an administration order is in force. No accounting period may be longer than 18 months.

References above to other group companies will include an holding company or subsidiary company incorporated overseas provided it has been incorporated in a country of the European Economic Area. The European Economic Area comprises the European Community plus Norway, Iceland and Liechtenstein.

Companies House will reject accounts which have not been made up to the Accounting Reference Date which they have on file. It is strongly advised, therefore, to ensure that some acknowledgement of receipt by Companies House of a change of Accounting Reference Date is received. This may be done by sending a covering letter in duplicate with a stamped addressed envelope requesting that the duplicate letter be returned as acknowledgement of receipt or by ensuring that Companies House standard letter DEB 79 confirming the period which the next accounts must cover has been received.

3:3   Composition of statutory Accounts

A company's Accounts comprise:

- **Profit and Loss Account – in the case of a holding company this will be a consolidated Account.**

- **Balance Sheet.**

- **Consolidated Balance Sheet – in the case of a holding company and this is in addition to the Balance Sheet for the holding company itself.**

- **Directors' Report.**

- **Auditors' Report (but see below with regard to small company audit exemption and dormant companies).**

A company's Accounts are not complete and do not comply with the Act if any of these documents are omitted. If the Accounts are not complete they are non-statutory Accounts and must comply with the publication requirements of s. 240 (s.10, CA 1989).

3:4 Directors' responsibility to prepare Accounts

It is the Directors' responsibility to ensure that Accounts are prepared in accordance with the detailed provisions of the Act and the various Accounting Standards which have been issued (s.226 (s.4, CA 1989)).

3:4.1 Approval of Accounts

Section 233 (s.7, CA 1989) further requires that:

(a) a company's Accounts shall be approved by the Board and the Balance Sheet shall be signed by a Director. (It is good practice that the approval of the Board of the company's Accounts be minuted in the appropriate Board minutes);

(b) every copy of the Balance Sheet shall state the name of the Director who signed on behalf of the Board;

(c) the copy of the Balance Sheet delivered to the Registrar shall carry a live signature.

3:4.2 Approval of Directors' Report

Section 234 (s.8, CA 1989) states that every company shall prepare a Directors' Report covering the matters set out in the attached schedule. Section 234A (s.8, CA 1989) requires that:

(a) the Directors' Report shall be approved by the Board and signed by a Director or by the Secretary. (Again, it is good practice that the approval by the Board of the Directors' Report be minuted in the appropriate Board minutes);

(b) every copy of the Directors' Report shall state the name of the person who signed the Report on behalf of the Board;

(c) the copy of the Report delivered to the Registrar shall carry a live signature.

3:4.3 Auditors' Report

Section 235 (s.9, CA 1989) sets out the Auditors' responsibility to report on the company's Accounts to the members, though certain small companies are now exempt from the requirement to have their accounts audited. Section 236 (s.9, CA 1989) requires that:

(a)   the Auditors' Report shall state the name of the Auditors and be signed by them;

(b)   every copy of the Auditors' Report shall state the names of the Auditors;

(c)   the copy of the Auditors' Report delivered to the Registrar shall state the names of the Auditors and carry a live signature.

3:4.4 Signatures on Accounts

It is emphasised that the signatures on the copies of the Balance Sheet, Directors' Report and Auditors' Report submitted to Companies House must be live signatures and that photocopies will not suffice. Care should be taken to ensure that where a document has been signed in black biro that it is clear that it is a live signature and not a photocopy.

3:5 Publication of Accounts

Having produced its Accounts the company must publish them at least to the extent set out in the following regulations:

(a)   send a copy to every member, debenture holder and every person entitled to receive notices of general meetings not less than 21 days before the meeting at which they are going to be laid (s.238 (s.10, CA 1989));

(b)   upon request, supply a copy of the latest Accounts to any member or debenture holder free of charge within seven days of being so requested (s.239 (s.10, CA 1989));

(c)   lay the Accounts before a general meeting within the time limits set out in s.244 and which are listed below (s.241 (s.11, CA 1989));

(d)   file the Accounts with the Registrar within the time limits set out in s.244 (s.242 (s.11, CA 1989)).

3:6 Time limits for laying and filing Accounts

The time limits set down in s.244 (s.11, CA 1989) for laying and filing Accounts are:

- **Private company – ten months after the end of the accounting reference period.**

- **Public company – seven months after the end of the accounting reference period.**

Where a company has overseas interests it may request an extension of three months to these time limits by submitting Form 244 to the Registrar prior to their normal expiry date.

In the case of a new company whose first accounting period exceeds 12 months then the time limits will be reduced correspondingly by the amount of time by which the accounting period exceeds 12 months but so that there is always at least three months available to file the Accounts. In these cases the time limit of ten months or seven months runs from the anniversary of the date of incorporation.

3:7 Penalties for late filing

If the Accounts are not filed in accordance with these time limits then, in addition to any criminal proceedings which may be instigated against the Directors, civil penalties will automatically be applied by Companies House under s.242A (s.11, CA 1989). These penalties range from an initial sum of £100 where the period that the accounts are late does not exceed three months to £1,000 where the period that the accounts are late exceeds 12 months in the case of a private company and from £500 to £5,000 respectively in the case of a public company.

Care must be taken where the Accounting Reference Date is 28 February or 30 April, June, September or November. The time limit for filing the Accounts will expire on the 28th or 30th of the appropriate month and not on the 31st of the month if applicable.

Companies House has announced that in the circumstances set out below it will consider on a case by case basis waiving a late filing penalty:

(a)　where accounts originally filed on time have to be returned to the company for amendment and are returned to Companies House within 14 days;

(b)　where accounts are filed up to three days late and there is no previous history of a late filing penalty being imposed.

3:8　Revision of incorrect Accounts

If it is found that the Accounts do not comply with the provisions of the Act in some material respect and those Accounts have been laid before the members or filed with the Registrar then a procedure for altering them is laid down in s.245 (s.12, CA 1989). The revisions, where minor, may be contained in a supplementary statement but otherwise a complete set of revised Accounts will have to be prepared.

3:8.1　Extent of revisions

The revisions must be confined to correcting those items which do not comply with the requirements of the Act and any consequential amendments. They must not be revised to encompass other information which has come to light since the original publication.

3:8.2　Auditors' Report on revisions

The Auditors will be required to certify the revised figures which must then be sent to everyone entitled to receive a copy of the Accounts. The revised Accounts will be laid before the next general meeting called by the company whether an Extraordinary General Meeting or an Annual General Meeting.

3:9　Abbreviated Accounts

A company which comes within the definition of a small or medium-sized company may file abbreviated Accounts with the Registrar although it must still send to its members and debenture holders Accounts which comply in all respects with the requirements of the Act (ss.246, 247, 248,

249 (s.13, CA 1989)). For small companies restricted accounts may also be sent to members as provided for in SI 1997 No. 220. These concessions do NOT apply to:

- **Public companies.**

- **Banking or Insurance companies.**

- **Companies authorised under the Financial Services Act 1986.**

- **Companies which are members of a group which contains an ineligible company.**

3:9.1 Eligibility to file abbreviated Accounts

To be eligible as a small or medium-sized company it is necessary to satisfy two of the three criteria set out below for the current financial year and the previous financial year or for a newly formed company for its first financial year.

3:9.1.1 Small company

Turnover	Not more than £2.8 million
Balance Sheet total	Not more than £1.4 million
Number of employees	Not more than 50.

3:9.1.2 Medium-sized company

Turnover	Not more than £11.2 million
Balance Sheet total	Not more than £5.6 million
Number of employees	Not more than 250.

The financial limits are under review and are likely to increase substantially.

3:9.2 Summary financial statements

Many public companies produce their Annual Report and Accounts as part of a high quality publication which is expensive to produce and mail. It is known that a large proportion of these publications are never read and the costs therefore unnecessarily incurred are high. Regulations have been made to combat this waste by allowing public companies whose shares or debentures are quoted on the Stock Exchange to issue summary financial statements but a full set of accounts may be requested by anyone entitled to receive them and must be supplied by the company.

3:10   Dispensing with laying Accounts

A private company may by elective resolution dispense with laying its Report and Accounts before a general meeting of members (s.252 (s.16, CA 1989)). Such a resolution has effect for the financial year in which it is passed and for succeeding years.

3:10.1   Requirement to dispatch Accounts

Where such an election is in force the company must send a copy of its Accounts to everyone entitled to receive them not less than 28 days before the last day for laying and filing Accounts. There should be included with the Accounts a statement to the effect that any member may require the Directors to convene a general meeting to consider those Accounts.

3:10.2   Requisition to lay Accounts

Within 28 days of dispatch of the Accounts any member or the Auditors may give notice in writing at the Registered Office of the company requiring the Accounts to be laid before a general meeting of members. The Directors must convene such a meeting within 21 days and the meeting must be held within a further 28 days.

3:10.3   Failure to lay Accounts

If the Directors fail to convene the meeting then the persons depositing the notice may convene the meeting themselves and it must be held within three months of the deposit of their notice. Any costs incurred in calling such a meeting may be recovered from the company which shall recoup them from any monies due to the Directors who were at fault in not calling the meeting (s.253 (s.16, CA 1989)).

3:11   Dormant companies

A dormant company is one which does not have any financial transactions to pass through its books during a financial year, except that a newly formed company whose only accounting transactions are the record of the receipt of money subscribed for the issue of shares as set out in the Memorandum will still be regarded as being dormant.

3:11.1 Ability to dispense with Auditors

Under s.250 (s.14, CA 1989) a dormant company may dispense with the need to appoint Auditors. Under SI 1997 No. 936 it is made clear that dormant companies may claim exemption from audit under the Audit Exemption Regulations (*see* **Para. 3:12**) as well as under s.250.

3:11.2 Eligibility to dispense with Auditors

To be eligible for this concession the company must be within the definition of a small company as stated above though it may be a member of a group; it may be a public or private company; it may not be a banking or insurance company or be authorised under the Financial Services Act 1986.

3:11.3 Procedure to dispense with Auditors

To avail itself of this concession the company must pass a special resolution not to appoint Auditors. If the company has been dormant since the end of the last financial year the special resolution may be passed at a general meeting at any time after the Accounts for that year have been dispatched to members. If the company has been dormant since incorporation then it may pass a similar special resolution prior to the Accounts for the first year being laid before the members.

Amendments to the regulations have been introduced whereby these resolutions may be passed as written resolutions.

3:11.4 Dormant company Accounts

Although the company may be dormant and excused from the obligation to appoint Auditors it must still produce, lay and file a Directors' Report and Accounts. The Accounts must also contain a statement on the Balance Sheet immediately above the Director's signature to the effect that the company has been dormant throughout the financial year. A dormant company must still file an Annual Return each year.

3:12 Audit exemption

Under the Companies Act 1985 (Audit Exemption) Regulations 1994 (SI 1994 No. 1935) a company may qualify for exemption from the need to have its accounts audited or may qualify to have an accountant's report (sometimes known as a compilation report) instead of an audit report.

3:12.1 Qualification for audit exemption

Section 249A, subs (1), states that for a company to qualify for total exemption from the audit regulations, or to qualify for an accountant's report, in any one year it must satisfy the following conditions:

(a)   it qualifies as a small company under s.246 (*see* **Para. 3:9.1.1**);

(b)   its balance sheet total for that year is not more than £1.4 million;

(c)   its turnover, or for a charitable company its gross income, satisfies the criteria set out below:

    i)   Total exemption

- **Turnover not exceeding £350,000 – For a non-charitable company for any accounting year.**

- **Gross Income not exceeding £90,000 – A company which is a charity for any accounting year.**

    ii)   Accountant's report

- **Gross Income exceeding £90,000 but not exceeding £250,000 – A company which is a charity for any accounting year.**

3:12.2 Restrictions on audit exemption

Under s.249B these exemptions from the need to have an audit report in any one year are not available if at any time during that year:

(a)   the company was a public company;

(b)   it was a banking or insurance company;

(c)   it was enrolled in the list maintained by the Insurance Brokers Registration Council;

(d) it was an authorised person or an appointed representative under the Financial Services Act 1986;

(e) it was a special register body or an employers' association under the Trade Union and Labour Relations (Consolidation) Act 1992;

(f) it was a parent company or a subsidiary unless it came within one of the exceptions mentioned below.

Where a newly formed company was a subsidiary of a registration agent and was dormant until sold by that registration agent it will not be debarred from audit exemption on account of that period as a subsidiary. Where the turnover of a group of companies comes within the limits for audit exemption the individual companies will then be eligible for the exemption.

3:12.3 Members' demand for an audit

Section 249B, subs. (2), enables a member or members to demand that the accounts for a financial year be audited by depositing a notice in writing at the Registered Office of the company not less than one month before the end of the financial year. The demand must be supported by holders of not less than ten per cent of the issued capital or any class thereof, or if the company does not have a share capital then by not less than ten per cent of the members.

3:12.4 Statement to be made on Balance Sheet

Where a company takes advantage of these exemptions it must have a statement on its balance sheet immediately above the signature that:

(a) for the year in question the company was entitled to exemption under subs. (1) or (2) (as the case may be) of s.249A, (*see* **Para. 3:12.1** above);

(b) no notice has been deposited under subs. (2) of s.249B in relation to its accounts for that financial year, (*see* **Para. 3:12.3** above);

(c) the Directors acknowledge their responsibilities for:

  (i)   ensuring that the company keeps accounting records which comply with s.221 (*see* **Para. 3:1**);

  (ii) preparing accounts which give a true and fair view of the state of affairs of the company as at the end of the financial year and of its profit or loss for the financial year in accordance with the requirements of s.226 (*see* **Para. 3:4**) and which otherwise comply with the requirements of the Act relating to accounts.

Where the company has an accountant's report it must be prepared by a person otherwise eligible for appointment as an auditor to a company or who is a member of the Association of Accounting Technicians, the Association of International Accountants or the Chartered Institute of Management Accountants and s.249C requires that the report shall state whether in the opinion of that accountant:

(a) the accounts of the company for the financial year are in agreement with the accounting records kept by the company under s.221;

(b) those accounts have been drawn up in a manner consistent with the provisions of the Act.

The report must also state that in the opinion of the accountant the company satisfied the financial limits for audit exemption and was not a company debarred under s.249B. The report must state the name of the accountant and be signed by him/her.

It has also been proposed that a prominent notice should be displayed on the front of the copy of the accounts delivered to the Registrar of any accounts which have not been subjected to audit. It is suggested that 'ACCOUNTS NOT SUBJECT TO AUDIT' or 'ACCOUNTS SUBJECT TO REPORT BY REPORTING ACCOUNTANT' as appropriate would be suitable.

3:13 Dispensing with the need to appoint Auditors

Where a company is exempt from the need to have its accounts audited either by being dormant or by the provisions set out in **Para. 3:12** above it need not appoint auditors. If, though, it is subsequently found that auditors are required they may be appointed by the Directors at any time prior to the meeting at which the accounts are to be laid and will hold office until the conclusion of that meeting (s.388A).

3:14   Directors' Report

The requirements regarding the matters to be disclosed in the Directors' Report are set out in s.234 (s.8, CA 1989) and Sch. 7 as amended by Sch. 5, CA 1989. It is the obligation of the Directors to prepare a Report for each financial year of the company and the matters to be included in that Report are as set out below:

(a)   a fair review of the development of the business of the company and its subsidiaries during the financial year and their position at the end of that year;

(b)   the amount of any dividend which it is recommended should be paid;

(c)   the names of those persons who have been Directors of the company at any time during the financial year;

(d)   the principal activities of the company and its subsidiaries during the year and any significant change in those activities during that year;

(e)   if the company has interests in land where the market value of those interests exceeds the book value to an extent which, in the opinion of the Directors is material, then this fact should be stated together with a reasonable estimate of the excess;

(f)   for every person who was a Director at the end of the year there shall be given details of any shares or debentures which he holds in the company or any other member of the group of which the company is a member. The information to be shown must state the holdings at the end of the financial year and also at the beginning of that year or at the date the Director was appointed if appointed during the year. If the Director has any rights to subscribe for shares in the company or other member of the group this must be stated together with details of any rights granted or exercised during the year. To the individual holdings must be added the holdings of the Director's spouse and any dependent children unless those persons are themselves Directors of the company. All of this information may be shown by way of a note to the Accounts as opposed to being shown in the Directors' Report itself if desired;

(g)   where a company which is not a wholly owned subsidiary of a company incorporated in Great Britain has given money for charitable or political purposes in excess of £200 during the financial year, it must state the charitable purpose and the amount donated or the name of the person given money for political purposes or the name of the political party and the amount given. In the case of a group of companies the information shall be given where the holding company and the subsidiaries between them contributed more than £200;

(h) details of any significant events which have occurred within the company or its subsidiaries since the year end and of any likely future developments in their businesses;

(i) an indication of any activities in the field of research and development by the company or its subsidiaries;

(j) where a company has acquired any of its own shares or shares are acquired by another person with financial assistance from the company and the company has a beneficial interest in those shares, there shall be stated the reason for the purchase, the number and nominal value of the shares concerned, the consideration paid and the percentage of the called–up capital of that class of shares that they represent;

(k) if the company has on average employed more than 250 people each week throughout the financial year it must state its policy with regard to the employment, training, career development and promotion of disabled people;

(l) for public companies and subsidiaries of public companies which do not come within the scope of small or medium sized companies there must be stated the company's policy on the payment of creditors, and also their practice in the form of the number of days creditors outstanding at the year end;

(m) if the company has on average employed more than 250 people each week throughout the financial year it must state the actions taken to inform and consult the workforce on matters of concern to them, to encourage their involvement in the performance of the company and to achieve awareness amongst the workforce of the financial and economic factors affecting the performance of the company;

(n) other than for an unlimited company, an indication of the existence of branches outside the UK.

■ CHECK LIST ■

Is the Accounting Reference Date correct for the company's needs? ☐

Are arrangements in hand to prepare the Accounts in time for filing? ☐

If the company has overseas interests:

(a) are returns received at least every six months? ☐

(b) has extra time been claimed for filing accounts? ☐

Do the Accounts contain all the necessary documents and comply with the Act? ☐

Is the Audit Report satisfactory and signed? ☐

Have the Accounts and Directors' Report been approved by the Board and signed? ☐

Do copies going to Companies House have live signatures on the Balance Sheet(s), Directors' Report and Audit Report? ☐

What is the latest date for circulating Accounts to the members? ☐

What is the latest date for laying the Accounts before a general meeting? ☐

Has an elective resolution been passed to dispense with laying Accounts before a general meeting and has a note been included with the Accounts circulated to members informing them of their right to demand that the Accounts be laid before a general meeting? ☐

Have Accounts been filed on time and has a check been made that they have been received by Companies House and that penalties are not being incurred? ☐

Is the company entitled to file abbreviated accounts? ☐

Is the company entitled to issue summary financial statements? ☐

■ CHECK LIST ■

Can the company dispense with an audit? ☐

If the company has decided to dispense with an audit,
is it still eligible? ☐

Filing Accounts and Annual Return

■ **CHAPTER FOUR** ■

Contents

■ KEY QUESTIONS ■

What returns have to be made to Companies House?

What are the time limits for filing the Annual Return?

What information has to be entered on the Annual Return?

What happens if the information supplied by Companies House is incorrect?

What happens if a new Director or Secretary has not been notified to Companies House?

What are the time limits for filing the Annual Report and Accounts?

Can the company claim an extension of time for overseas interests?

Are there penalties for late filing of the Annual Report and Accounts?

What other documents have to be filed with Companies House?

What are the printing requirements for documents to be filed?

How can the company obtain an acknowledgement of receipt for documents filed at Companies House?

From where are Companies Act forms obtained?

4:1 Annual requirements for filing

Every company must each year file with the Registrar an Annual Return (Form 363) and a copy of its Annual Report and Accounts. If the Registrar does not receive these documents within the stipulated time limits then he will take action to ensure compliance. As a last resort he will, if necessary, arrange for summonses to be issued against the Directors of the company and if found guilty the accused will not only have a criminal record but will also face a fine of up to £5,000 and a continuing default fine for non–compliance of up to £500 per day.

4:2 Time limits for Annual Return

The time limit for filing the Annual Return is defined by the latest date to which it must be made up and it must be received by Companies House within 28 days of that date. The latest date for making up the Annual Return will be the anniversary of the date to which the last year's return was compiled or in the case of a newly formed company the anniversary of the date of incorporation. It will be considered to have been filed on time if it is received by the due date, that is 28 days after the date to which it is made up, either at Companies House in Cardiff, for companies registered in England and Wales, or in Edinburgh, for companies registered in Scotland, or in one of the satellite offices established by the Registrar in London, Birmingham, Leeds and Manchester for companies registered in England and Wales and in Glasgow for companies registered in Scotland.

4:3 Choice of alternative date

If a company wishes to make up its Annual Return to a date other than the latest date as established by the rules set out in **4:2** above it may do so. If the date desired is earlier in the year than the latest date, it may file its Annual Return made up to the desired date and provided it is received by Companies House within 28 days of that date then it will be accepted as the Annual Return for that year. It is emphasised, however, that it must be received by Companies House or by one of its satellite offices within the specified time limits and no allowances can be made for delays in delivery, no matter how they may be caused.

Once accepted by Companies House as the Annual Return for the year then it will establish a new base date for calculating the latest date for the following year's Annual Return.

If the company wishes to establish a date later in the year than the current latest date for filing its Annual Return it will be necessary to make up an Annual Return to the latest date as detailed in **4:2** above, or some earlier date and then file a second Annual Return made up to the desired date. This second Annual Return must be filed within 28 days of the date to which it is made up and once accepted by Companies House as an Annual Return then it will form a new base date for calculating the subsequent year's latest date.

4:4   Contents of Annual Return

The Annual Return is now a shuttle document (Form 363s) issued individually by Companies House to each company registered and showing on that document the information currently recorded on the Companies House files. The information should be altered where necessary, any additional information entered, signed by the Secretary or a Director and returned to the Registrar with a remittance for £15. It is still possible to submit an Annual Return by completing a blank Annual Return Form 363a or a Form generated by a secretarial software package.

A revised Form 363s came into force for all return dates on or after 28 September 1999. This return no longer requires the other directorships of the Directors to be shown nor any former names which they may have used. A private company also no longer has to show whether it has passed elective resolutions to dispense with holding Annual General Meetings or to dispense with laying the Annual Report and Accounts before a General Meeting. For companies with up to 20 members which have previously submitted an Annual Return there will now be shown the list of members taken from the previous year's Annual Return and the issued capital. For most other companies which have previously submitted an Annual Return there will now be shown the issued capital. For the largest companies (approximately 3,000 in number) neither the membership list nor the capital will be pre-printed on the form.

The contents of the Annual Return are:

(a)   the company name;

(b)   the company type (e.g. private company limited by shares);

(c)   the company number;

(d)   the address of the Registered Office;

(e)   the address where the Register of Members is kept if not at the Registered Office;

(f)   the address where a Register of Debenture Holders is kept if not at the Registered Office;

(g)   the principal business activities of the company. These activities are defined by a series of codes similar to the standard industrial classification codes;

(h)   details of the Company Secretary;

(i)   details of the Directors;

(j)   details of the issued share capital;

(k)   a list of members (*see* **section 4:6**);

(l)   the date to which the return is made up. There will be shown in section 2 of the Declaration the latest date to which the return may be made up. If this date is being used as the make up date for this return no further entries in respect of dates need be made. If, however, the return is being made up to a different date to the latest date available the date used should be entered in the appropriate space in section 2. If a date is required for the next return which is not the anniversary of the date to which this return has been made up then the date required should be entered in section 3 of the Declaration. This will alert Companies House to send a shuttle Annual Return at the appropriate time and when a return has been made up to this new date and been accepted by Companies House it will form a new base date for determining the latest date to which the next year's return may be made up.

4:5   Revision of detail provided by Companies House

If it is found that any information concerning:

(a)   the address of the Registered Office;

(b)   the address where a Register of Members is kept;

(c)   the address where a Register of Debenture Holders is kept;

(d)   particulars of a Director including no longer holding office;

(e)   particulars of the Company Secretary including no longer holding office,

is incorrect on the document produced by Companies House (Form 363s) the company may alter it and Companies House will accept notification in this manner and the appropriate form specified in the Act need not be submitted. Companies House do state, however, that they will take action if they find this concession is being abused.

Should it be found that the appointment of a Director or the Company Secretary has not been notified to Companies House then Form 288a will still have to be submitted and the details will not be accepted from an amended Annual Return Form. This is because a new Director or Company Secretary must sign Form 288a to signify acceptance of the appointment.

It is emphasised that acceptance of changes of information from the Annual Return Form is only permitted where the shuttle form 363s is used. If a Form 363a or a form generated by a computer company secretarial package is used then any change of information must be separately notified to Companies House on the appropriate form. The appropriate forms are:

(a)   Form 287 – Change of address of the Registered Office;

(b)   Form 353 – Change of address where the Register of Members is kept if not at the Registered Office;

(c)   Form 190 – Change of address where the Register of Debenture Holders is kept if not at the Registered Office;

(d)   Form 288a – Appointment of a new Director or Company Secretary;

(e)   Form 288b – Resignation or removal of a Director or Company Secretary;

(f)   Form 288c – Change in the particulars of a Director or Company Secretary.

Any changes to the issued share capital must be notified to Companies House on the appropriate form, which for an allotment of shares is Form 88(2).

4:6   List of members

Where a company receives an Annual Return upon which is pre-printed the list of members, it will show for each member the holding of shares split between the various classes of share if applicable. Any alterations to that list should be noted so that Companies House records may be updated. Where a member has disposed of all or part of their holding, the number of shares held must be amended and there should be entered against the name of that member details of the number of shares transferred and the date of transfer.

For a company whose membership list is not pre-printed on the Annual Return a full list of members must be provided every third year. In intervening years a list of changes need only be provided every third year. In intervening years a list of changes need only be provided or the box be ticked on the Annual Return to say that there had been no changes during the year. Where a list of members is sent to Companies House the Annual Return should show in the appropriate box whether that list is on paper or in computer readable form. The detail which has to be shown for each member is the same as shown above for companies whose membership list is pre-printed.

4:7 Time limits for Annual Report and Accounts

The Annual Report and Accounts must be filed with the Registrar each year and there is no official document to accompany them and no filing fee is required. In the case of a private company they must be filed within ten months of the Accounting Reference Date and in the case of a public company within seven months of the Accounting Reference Date. If the company has overseas interests a three months' extension to these time limits may be claimed by submitting to the Registrar Form 244. This form must be submitted prior to the expiry of the original time limit.

It should be noted that where the accounting reference period ends on 28 February or 30 April, June, September or November the time limit for filing will expire on the 28th or 30th of the appropriate month and not on the 31st of that month.

In the case of a newly formed company whose first accounting period exceeds 12 months the time allowed for filing is reduced by the amount of time the accounting period exceeds 12 months but it shall never be reduced to less than three months. The period allowed for filing will in these cases run from the anniversary of the date of incorporation.

Due to the late filing penalties for overdue accounts (*see* **Para. 4:8**) it is recommended that a receipt is always requested when filing the Annual Report and Accounts (*see* **Para. 4:11**).

4:8 Penalties for late filing

If the Annual Report and Accounts are not filed on time Companies House will automatically apply civil penalties laid down in the Act in s.242A(2) (s.11, CA 1989). As with the Annual Return the documents must be delivered to Companies House or one of its satellite offices within the prescribed period and any delay, despite whatever valid reason may exist for it, will be penalised.

The penalties for a private company range from £100 for up to three months overdue to £1,000 for over 12 months overdue and for a public company from £500 to £5,000 respectively, and will apply immediately the accounts are overdue for filing with no days of grace allowed. However, Companies House has announced some limited concessions as set out in **Para. 3:7**.

These penalties are in addition to any criminal proceedings which may be commenced against the Directors as described above.

4:9 Other documents to be filed

In addition to the Annual Return and the Annual Report and Accounts many other returns have to be filed with the Registrar should the company carry out certain actions specified in the Act. Those returns have to be made on the appropriate form which will be numbered according to the section of the Act specifying the information which has to be supplied to the Registrar. The majority of those returns have to be made within 14/15 days of the happening of the particular event except for the registration of charges where 21 days are allowed and returns of the issue of shares or the purchase by a company of its own shares where 28 days are allowed.

4:9.1 Filing copy resolutions

By s.380 as amended by s.116, CA 1989 copies of all special, extraordinary and elective resolutions and resolutions revoking elective resolutions must be filed with the Registrar within 15 days of being passed. Only in those circumstances where specifically provided in the Act will ordinary resolutions be filed, again within 15 days of being passed. Copies of resolutions must be in accordance with the general regulations for filing documents as set out below and be signed by a Director or by the Company Secretary.

4:10   Document quality

Companies House will refuse to accept documents for filing which are indistinct or of poor quality and which are unsuitable for microfilming. Their requirements for documents submitted for filing are:

(a)   A4 in size;

(b)   on white or near white matt paper. If the Annual Report and Accounts are produced as part of a glossy booklet it will be necessary to obtain a printers' proof or typed copy on matt paper for filing;

(c)   contain the company name and the company number which must be in a prominent position. It is suggested that if possible the company number should be shown on the top right hand corner of the front page. This should be borne in mind when submitting the Annual Report and Accounts which will generally be produced without the company number being shown;

(d)   have a margin of 10mm and if bound a margin of 20mm on the bound edge;

(e)   have letters and numbers of at least 1.8mm in height with a line width of at least 0.25mm;

(f)   letters and numbers must be clear, legible and of uniform density.

4:11   Acknowledgement of receipt

Companies House will not send out acknowledgements of receipt for documents submitted to them for filing. If a receipt is required it is necessary to send with the documents a covering letter in duplicate and a stamped self-addressed envelope. Companies House will then receipt the duplicate of the covering letter and return it to the presentor of the documents.

It is suggested that it is advisable to ask for a receipt where the time limits for filing are critical as when submitting an Annual Return made up to a date other than the latest date and when filing the Annual Report and Accounts. When filing a change of Accounting Reference Date on Form 225 a receipt will be supplied automatically by Companies House and a watch must be kept to ensure it is received.

4:12　Obtaining Companies Act forms

Copies of all the forms specified for use in the Companies Acts are obtainable from Companies House free of charge. They can be collected over the counter from Companies House in Cardiff or Edinburgh or from any of the satellite offices or they will be sent by post in response to a telephone, letter or fax request. They can also be purchased from various commercial legal stationers.

■ CHECK LIST ■

Has the Annual Return shuttle document been
received from Companies House? ☐

To what date is Annual Return going to be made up? ☐

What is the latest date for filing the Annual Return? ☐

What arrangements are being made to ensure
it is received by Companies House in time? ☐

Are the contents of the Annual Return correct
and have amendments been made where necessary? ☐

Are there any appointments of Directors or Secretary
which have not been recorded and have Forms 288a
been prepared for submission? ☐

Is the list of members up-to-date? ☐

What is the latest date for filing the Annual
Report and Accounts? ☐

Does the company need to claim an extension for
overseas interests? ☐

Has the company number been entered on the front
page of the accounts? ☐

Has a check been made that the Accounts have been
received by Companies House and that penalties
are not being incurred? ☐

Are all other filing requirements especially copies
of all special, extraordinary and elective
resolutions up-to-date? ☐

Are all documents to be filed suitable for microfilming? ☐

■ CHAPTER FIVE ■

Share transfers

■ CHAPTER FIVE ■

Contents

■ KEY QUESTIONS ■

How does a member request the company to transfer shares registered in his name?

Are share transfers liable to stamp duty?

Can the Directors refuse to register a transfer?

What has to be done when a share transfer form is received?

What happens if a member dies?

How quickly do share certificates have to be issued?

Can the company issue a replacement for a lost share certificate?

5:1   Introduction

Whenever a shareholder makes a request to a company that some or all of the shares registered in his/her name be transferred to another person that request should be on a properly completed share transfer form and be accompanied by the appropriate share certificate.

5:2   Stamp duty

Prior to registering the transfer the transfer form must be stamped by the Inland Revenue or be certified on the reverse of the form by the transferee that the transaction comes within one of the classes listed there as not being liable to stamp duty.

5:3   Directors' powers to refuse a transfer of shares

If the company is a private company and the Directors have the power bestowed upon them through the Articles to refuse to register a transfer of shares if they so desire then the approval of the Board must be sought before further action is taken on transferring the shares. If the Directors do decide to exercise their powers and refuse to sanction a particular transfer then they must follow the procedures laid down precisely. Their powers in this respect come from the Articles and their failure to abide by the conditions set down in the Articles would prevent them from using those powers to prevent a transfer taking place.

5:4   Verification of transfer documents

When a share transfer is presented for registration the documents must be carefully checked to see that they concur with the information on the company's records. Any differences in the transferors' names or their spelling or address should be clarified and the share certificate should be checked to see that it accords with the company's records and covers the shares to be transferred.

5:5 Register of Share Transfers

When it is satisfactorily concluded that the transfer appears to be in order, the share certificate should be cancelled and the details of the transfer entered in the Register of Share Transfers. This Register will show the following details:

(a) date of entry of the transfer;

(b) name of transferor;

(c) number and class of shares to be transferred;

(d) number of share certificate(s) returned and now cancelled;

(e) name and address of the transferee(s);

(f) number of shares to be taken by the transferee(s);

(g) consideration for the transfer.

5:6 Registration of transfer in Register of Members

An entry should then be made in the account in the Register of Members of the transferor removing from his/her holding those shares now being transferred. Similarly, an entry should be made in the account in the Register of Members of the transferee, setting up a new account if necessary, adding to his/her holding those shares which have just been acquired. The account numbers of the transferor and transferee should be entered against the respective entries in the Register of Share Transfers.

5:7 Preparation of share certificates

Share certificates should then be prepared for the transferee(s) and for the transferor if a balance certificate is required as the certificate surrendered covered more shares than those being transferred, and they should then be presented for sealing. The share certificate numbers should also be entered in the Register of Share Transfers and in the respective accounts in the Register of Members. When sealed the share certificates should be dispatched to the shareholders or their agents.

5:8 Transmission of shares

Transmission of shares is not a transfer. Transmission of shares takes place when a shareholder has died and the shares are dealt with by the executors or the administrators of the estate. It is usual to comply with a request from an executor or an administrator to have the shares transferred into his/her own name as this is normally the most convenient course of action for the company. It is suggested that as a matter of convenience a request for transmission of shares should always be made on a share transfer form.

5:9 Probate

Production of probate or letters of administration, or in Scotland confirmation, impressed with the Court stamp should be accepted as sufficient evidence of their grant despite anything to the contrary which may be contained in the Articles (s.187).

5:10 Issue of share certificates

Share or debenture certificates should be issued within two months of allotment or the lodgment of a share transfer and if the Directors of a private company are exercising their right to refuse to register a transfer they must notify the transferee within two months of the lodgment of the transfer. The Articles may prescribe shorter time limits than those set out in the Act.

5:11 Changes in shareholder details

Care should be taken when a change of address is registered to ensure that it is legitimate and initiated by the lawful owner of the shares and should have reference to the address held on the company's records and the new address. A change of name should be accompanied by documentary evidence. In a small private company where the shareholders are known personally to the Company Secretary this level of formality is probably not justified but care should always be taken.

5:12 Lost share certificates

If a share or debenture certificate has been lost an indemnity should be sought from the holder before a duplicate is issued. In the case of a public company this indemnity should be from a Bank or an insurance company but this level of protection is probably not justified in the case of a small private company. Even in a private company though a letter should be obtained from the shareholder undertaking to indemnify the company should any loss be incurred by the company by the issue of a duplicate certificate.

■ CHECK LIST ■

Are all share transfer requests made on proper
    share transfer forms? ☐

Are all transfers stamped or certified not liable to
    stamp duty? ☐

Do the Directors have a right to refuse a transfer
    request and do they exercise it? ☐

Are details on the Register of Members up-to-date
    and are share transfers checked against them? ☐

Is a register of share transfers kept? ☐

Is there a procedure for posting share transfers
    to the Register of Members and for preparing
    share certificates? ☐

Is there a policy for dealing with holdings of
    deceased members? ☐

Are share certificates issued within the time limits? ☐

Is there a procedure for dealing with changes in
    membership details? ☐

Does the company have a standard letter of
    indemnity to be signed when a member requests
    a duplicate share certificate? ☐

Payment of dividends

■ CHAPTER SIX ■

Contents

■ KEY QUESTIONS ■

Are there any limitations on the amount of dividend which may be paid?

Are there similar restrictions on the payment of debenture interest?

Can the Directors decide to pay dividends in a different order of preference to that set down in the Articles?

Who decides when a dividend may be paid?

Which shareholder receives the dividend if a transfer takes place shortly before the payment date?

What tax applies to debenture interest?

Does the dividend voucher have to be a printed document?

What has to be shown on the dividend voucher?

May dividends be paid directly into a member's Bank account?

What payments have to be made to the Inland Revenue in connection with an interest payment and when?

94

6:1 Limitation on dividend payments

A company may only pay a dividend on its shares out of realised profits. Those profits need not be accrued during the year for which the dividend is being paid but may be undistributed profits brought forward from previous years. In the case of a public company by s.264 a dividend may not be paid unless the company's net assets exceed the sum of the called-up capital and any undistributable reserves, and the dividend may not be of such a size that it would reduce the net assets below this figure. In the case of a public company which wishes to pay an interim dividend should the previous year's accounts not show sufficient undistributed profits to cover the proposed interim dividend then interim accounts showing sufficient profits to cover the dividend must be filed with the Registrar.

6:2 Payment of interest on debentures

The payments made in respect of debentures and loan stocks are interest and not dividends and therefore the restrictions whereby payments may only be made out of profits do not apply. This difference is also reflected in that interest is subject to income tax and dividends have attached to them a tax credit.

6:3 Dividend payments subject to the Articles

The payment of a dividend is also subject to the Articles of the company. Consideration needs to be given to the rights of the various types of share in issue, so that no dividend is declared on a particular class of share until due dividends have been paid on those classes of share which have preferred rights to dividend.

6:4 Approval of dividend by the members

The provisions in Table A concerning the payment of dividends are commonly followed and provide that if the Directors declare an interim dividend it may be paid without reference to the members, but a final dividend is subject to the approval of the members in general meeting. The members may approve the dividend recommended by the Directors or reduce the amount but may not increase it.

6:5 Date of payment

The Directors when declaring a dividend must also decide on the date of payment and the date on which a member has to be registered in the Register of Members to receive the payment. In the case of a public company they must also establish the date when dealings in the company's shares become ex-dividend. This date is established according to the Stock Exchange rules and determines when purchasers of those shares do not become entitled to the dividend which has been declared. For a private company where share dealing is infrequent it would normally be for the parties to a transaction to decide between themselves as to who was entitled to receive future dividends.

6:6 Calculation of amount payable

Once the dividend has been declared it will be necessary to prepare as at the registration date a list of members holding that particular class of share ensuring the total holdings equal the total number of shares in issue.

The dividend for each individual holding must then be calculated, rounding off as necessary to ensure that the total of the individual payments equals the amount of dividend calculated on the total number of shares in issue.

The tax credit has then to be calculated on each individual holding at the fraction published by the tax authorities which represents the tax that would have been deducted at the prescribed rate from a notional gross sum to give the net dividend which is being paid. Again, the individual amounts of tax credit must be rounded off to equal the calculation made on the total dividend.

With regard to debentures and loan stocks, similar calculations will be made for the gross interest, the deduction of income tax at the standard rate on the gross interest and the net payment due.

6:7   Preparation of dividend voucher

A dividend or interest voucher has to be prepared and in a large company this will obviously be printed, probably designed for direct output from a computer. In a small company this level of expense is probably not justified and a document designed in-house will suffice. This document must show the following information:

(a)   the name of the company. This should be the full name and not just the company logo;

(b)   the title of the security upon which the dividend or the interest is being paid;

(c)   the period in respect of which the dividend or interest is being paid;

(d)   the amount of the dividend or the rate of interest being paid;

(e)   the date of payment;

(f)   the holding upon which the dividend or the interest is being paid;

(g)   for dividends:

    (i)   the dividend being paid;

    (ii)   the tax credit attached to that dividend;

(h)   for interest:

    (i)   the gross interest;

    (ii)   the income tax deducted from that interest;

    (iii)   the net interest paid;

(i)   for interest payments, a statement signed by an officer of the company (usually the Secretary) undertaking to account to the Inland Revenue for the income tax shown.

6:8 Completion of dividend voucher

Where the Register of Members or Register of Debenture Holders is of sufficient size to be kept on a computer the dividend or interest vouchers will probably be produced with a cheque attached, where appropriate, and with Bank lists for those who have mandated their dividends or interest directly to their Bank accounts. Alternatively, the vouchers will have to be completed, the cheques drawn and the Bank lists prepared for those who have mandated their dividends or interest.

Vouchers and cheques, where applicable, can then be mailed to the members or debenture holders at the appropriate time.

6:9 Special arrangements with the paying Bank

In large companies it is not unusual for a separate Bank account to be opened solely to cater for the dividend payments. If this is to be the practice then the appropriate arrangements have to be made with the Bank and the cheques have to be printed.

6:10 Accounting to the Inland Revenue

The company must account to the Inland Revenue for the income tax deducted from the interest by submitting Form CT61 with the appropriate remittance by the 14th of the month following the end of the quarter ending on the last day of March, June, September or December in which the payment is made.

■ CHECK LIST ■

Are there profits available to cover the dividend? ☐

For a public company are the net assets of sufficient size to permit the dividend proposed? ☐

Have any restriction in the Articles with regard to the rights of other classes of share to participate in distributions of profit been satisfied? ☐

Is the approval of the members required prior to the payment of the dividend? ☐

Is the date of payment to be agreed by the Board? ☐

What is the registration date for payment? ☐

At what date will the shares go ex-dividend? ☐

Is the Register of Members up-to-date and can a list of shareholdings be easily extracted? ☐

Does the dividend voucher have to be printed and if so are arrangements in hand for this to be done as soon as the dividend is declared? ☐

Has the draft of the dividend voucher been prepared and checked in good time to ensure payment is made on due date? ☐

Are arrangements in hand for the completion of the dividend vouchers and the preparation of the cheques and Bank lists? ☐

Is a special Bank account required for the dividend payment? ☐

If the company pays debenture interest are arrangements in hand for the completion of the CT61 and for payment of the tax due to the Inland Revenue? ☐

Directors

Contents

■ KEY QUESTIONS ■

What is the definition of a Director?

Can the company call senior staff Directors even though they are not on the Board?

What is a Shadow Director?

How is a new Director appointed?

Do Directors have to retire by rotation?

Is there an age limit for Directors?

How can a Director be removed from office?

Is there a minimum number of Directors a company must have?

Do the names of Directors have to be shown on letterheading?

Can a Director appoint an alternate to act in his place?

What is the difference between an executive Director and a non-executive Director?

Do Directors have collective responsibility?

What are the duties of a Director?

Do Directors have to declare their outside interests?

If the company is a Single Member Company and the sole member is a Director what special provisions apply?

Can the company make loans to Directors?

Can the company indemnify a Director?

Can the company take out insurance to indemnify a Director?

Can a Director be disqualified from holding office?

Can a Director be liable for wrongful trading?

7:1 Definition of Director

Section 741 states that a Director is any person occupying that position by whatever name called. The Act therefore looks behind the name given and examines the actual relationship which the person has with the company to determine whether they are in fact a Director.

A Director is any person who has with others or on his own the ultimate responsibility of running the company. The details of all Directors should be recorded in the Register of Directors and Secretary and the information should be returned to Companies House on Form 288a.

7:1.1 Status not given simply by name

In some companies senior staff are given titles which encompass the word Director to give enhanced status when dealing with customers. These people will not be Directors solely through their title and would only be Directors if they were members of the Board and for whom Form 288a had been filed. If a member of the staff of the company has a title containing the word Director although he/she is not a member of the Board but exceeds his/her authority and commits the company as if he/she was a Director then the company will be prevented from denying to third parties that he/she was a Director.

7:1.2 Shadow Directors

Section 741 goes on to describe a Shadow Director as a person in accordance with whose directions or instructions the Directors are accustomed to act. Professional advisors and the holding company of a subsidiary are specifically excluded from this definition.

This definition has not been tested in the Courts and its meaning cannot be explained with certainty but it is felt that a person who habitually gives to the Directors good advice upon which they act will not necessarily be a Shadow Director. Where, however, advice, directions or instructions are given by a person who exercises some measure of control over the Directors, for example, through the control of funding of the company or who has voting control and who can remove the Directors from office may well come within the definition of a Shadow Director.

7:2   Appointment of a Director

The appointment of a Director must be in accordance with the Articles which usually provide for the Board to fill a casual vacancy or add to their number. A Director may be appointed by ordinary resolution at a general meeting of the company although Table A states that if proposed by a member special notice must be given to the company.

The appointment should be minuted in the appropriate Board or general meeting minutes, the details of the Director should be entered in the Register of Directors and Secretary and Form 288a, signed by the person appointed accepting the appointment, should be submitted to Companies House.

7:3   Retirement by rotation

Directors do not have to retire by rotation unless it is required by the Articles. If there is no such provision in the Articles then a Director once appointed remains in office until he/she retires or a resolution is passed to remove him/her from office.

Where Directors do retire by rotation it is usually provided that a Director will retire and be eligible to stand for re-election at the next Annual General Meeting following his/her appointment by the Board to fill a casual vacancy, or as an addition to their numbers, and that in addition one third of the Board will retire each year and be eligible for re-election. It is not normal for a person appointed to the position of Managing Director to retire by rotation.

7:4   Age limit for Directors

In a public company or a subsidiary of a public company by virtue of s.293 there is an age limit for Directors. The provisions require that:

(a)   no person aged over 70 may be appointed or reappointed a Director unless approved by the members in general meeting of which special notice has been given stating his/her age. Special notice has to be given to the company by a member;

(b)   a Director aged over 70 will retire at the next Annual General

Meeting following his/her 70th birthday, but will be eligible for re-election in accordance with the provisions above;

(c) a Director retiring on account of age does not affect the calculation of the one third of the Board retiring by rotation;

(d) a Director aged over 70 who is reappointed takes his/her normal turn in retiring by rotation and special notice will have to be given every time he/she comes up for re-election;

(e) if the Managing Director is aged over 70 and does not usually retire by rotation, once he/she has been reappointed when special notice was given stating his/her age there will be no further need for him/her to retire.

7:5 Removal of a Director

Under s.303 the members may remove a Director from office by ordinary resolution passed in a general meeting of which special notice has been given. The vacancy so created need not be filled at the meeting but may be filled by the Directors as a casual vacancy. If, however, a person is proposed to replace the Director who is being removed then special notice has to be given of his/her appointment. A person so appointed will take the place of the person removed in determining his/her turn to retire by rotation.

7:5.1 Rights of Director to be removed from office

If the company receives notice under s.303 that it is proposed that a Director be removed from office it must immediately inform the Director concerned. The Director has a right to be heard at the meeting whether or not he/she is a member and may also require a circular of reasonable length to be distributed to the members. The company or any aggrieved person may petition the Court for the circular to be suppressed if undue publicity is being given to defamatory material.

7:5.2 Removal of Director by Board

A provision in the Articles whereby the Directors have the power to remove one of their number from the Board is perfectly valid. It is generally felt to be beneficial to have such a provision in the Articles so that should a dispute arise which it is believed can only be resolved by the removal from the Board of some of their number this can be effected with the minimum of publicity.

7:5.3   Compensation for loss of office

Where a Director is removed under any of these provisions it does not deprive him/her of any rights he/she may have under a contract of service to compensation for the loss of his/her directorship and any executive position he/she may have held.

7:5.4   Record of resignation or removal

Where a Director resigns or is removed from office, his/her resignation or removal should be recorded in the appropriate Board minutes and Form 288b should be submitted to Companies House.

7:6   Sundry provisions regarding Directors

These include:

(a)   a public company must have at least two Directors and a private company must have at least one Director (s.282);

(b)   if the Articles specify that the Directors must hold a share qualification then it must be obtained within two months or such shorter time as specified in the Articles (s.291). Care should be taken though if this period coincides with the closed period for Director's share dealings as laid down by the Stock Exchange;

(c)   in a public company the Directors must be appointed individually unless previously a resolution has been passed with no-one voting against it that a combined resolution be moved (s.292);

(d)   the names of the Directors need not be shown on the letterheading but if any are printed then they must all be shown (s.305). This provision applies to names printed as part of the layout of the stationery and does not apply to names which appear as part of, or subscription to, correspondence;

(e)   a Director or Shadow Director is forbidden to deal in options in shares or debentures in his/her own company or associated companies (s.323). The options which are forbidden are those which give a right to deliver or call for delivery of shares or debentures and not those which give a right to subscribe for shares;

(f)   an undischarged bankrupt may not be a Director or involved in the management of a company (s.11, Company Directors Disqualification Act 1986);

(g)   a Director may appoint an Alternate Director to act in his/her place when he/she is absent if permitted by the Articles. The terms of the appointment will be governed by the Articles. An Alternate Director is a Director for Companies Act purposes and details of the person appointed must be recorded in the Register of Directors and Secretary and notified to Companies House on Form 288a.

7:7   Non-executive Directors

The Companies Acts do not differentiate between executive directors who have a full-time position with the company and non-executive directors who only have a part-time appointment with the company.

The terms of non-executive directors vary widely and may encompass a number of days' work each week or entail little more than attendance at Board meetings. Irrespective of the amount of involvement with the company all Directors are subject to the full provisions and penalties of the Acts.

7:8   Collective responsibility

Directors have a collective responsibility and if a member of the Board is in disagreement with the remainder of the Board over a matter of sufficient importance then his/her dissent should be minuted.

7:9 Directors' duties

Directors' duties could be said to fall within three headings:

(a) they must act within their powers as described in the Companies Acts and in the Articles;

(b) they must exercise care and act in the best interests of the company. This obligation can cause difficulties where a person is appointed a Director to represent the interests of certain shareholders and on a particular matter the best interests of the remainder of the shareholders differ from those of the shareholders represented by the Director;

(c) they must be aware of the fiduciary nature of their position and not use their powers to make a personal profit.

7:9.1 Fiduciary nature of position

In connection with this fiduciary position, a Director or Shadow Director must declare to the Board his/her outside interests. This can be done either by declaring all his/her interests at the time of appointment and ensuring that it is kept up-to-date, or by declaring his/her interest at the time should a relevant matter come before the Board (s.317).

7:9.2 Directors' interest in contracts

A Director may not participate in any Board discussion or decision on a contract in which he/she has a personal interest unless the Articles specifically provide otherwise. If the contract is of sufficient size and a Director has a personal interest in that contract it must go before a general meeting of members for approval prior to the company entering into that contract; the company must not enter into the contract and then go to the members for their confirmation.

If a contract does go before a general meeting of members the Director who has the personal interest may vote in favour of the resolution if he/she is a member as he/she is then voting as a member in his/her private capacity and not as a Director with obligations to the membership as a whole. A contract must be placed before a general meeting of members if it exceeds

£100,000 or ten per cent of the company's net asset value, whichever is the less, with a *de minimis* limit of £2,000 (s.320).

7:9.3 *Single member contracting with the company*

In a Single Member Company where the sole member is a Director or a Shadow Director and he/she contracts with the company in his/her personal capacity other than in the normal course of the company's business then if the contract is not in writing a written memorandum of its terms must be provided or the terms must be recorded in the minutes of the first meeting of Directors after the contract was concluded. Failure to do so does not invalidate the contract but does lay open the company and its Officers to penalties (s.322B (The Companies (Single Member Private Limited Companies) Regulations 1992 – SI 1992 No.1699)).

7:10   Loans to Directors

Under s.330, in general terms, a company must not make loans to its Directors. There are a number of exceptions to this general rule which are complicated and if there is a pressing need to make a loan to a Director the Act should be examined in detail to see whether any of the exceptions listed fit the circumstances of the particular case. The main exceptions of general application are:

(a)   inter-company loans between subsidiary and holding company;

(b)   small amounts up to £5,000;

(c)   advancing funds not exceeding £20,000 to meet expenditure to be incurred on company business. Vouchers for the expenditure incurred should be produced, and any surplus funds should be returned within a reasonable period, otherwise the advance could be construed as a loan;

(d)   normal credit transactions where the sum involved does not exceed £10,000.

There are restrictions attached to these general exceptions and the Act should be consulted if it is planned to take advantage of them.

7:11 Indemnity

A company may not indemnify a Director against negligence, default, breach of duty or breach of trust except in defending any proceedings where judgment is given in his/her favour or he/she is acquitted (s.310). If a Director is found guilty of any of the liabilities mentioned in either criminal or civil proceedings he/she will be personally liable for any fines or damages awarded and for his/her own costs and any other costs awarded against him/her. The company would not be allowed to indemnify him/her.

7:11.1 Directors' and Officers' Liability Insurance

The law has been clarified in s.137, CA 1989 so that it is now clear that a company may take out insurance (Directors' and Officers' Liability Insurance) to protect its officers from these liabilities. If insurance is carried it no longer has to be mentioned in the Annual Report Care should be taken if it is proposed to cover all Directors under a single policy as it could be said to be a contract in which the Director has a personal interest and there would not be a disinterested quorum at the Board Meeting to approve it, subject to the provisions of the company's Articles, thus necessitating approval by a general meeting. A series of policies each covering an individual Director would seem to be a preferable way of proceeding.

7:12 Liabilities of Directors

The terms negligence, default, breach of duty or breach of trust can have very wide meanings and it is difficult to define exactly all misdemeanours which would come within the scope of these terms. It would seem, however, that almost any act of a Director which subsequently is found to be flawed in some respect could come within their terms. Examples of items which could incur these liabilities are negligent advice, mis-statement of facts, unauthorised payments, imprudent investments, negligent supervision and errors of judgment. Directors can also be liable under various statutes and could find themselves answerable to the Health and Safety Executive, the Inland Revenue and Customs and Excise.

7:13 Disqualification from holding office

In addition to any fines that may be levied for breaches of the Companies Acts the Courts may in certain circumstances disqualify a Director from holding office or from being concerned in the management of a company.

The powers of the Court come from the Company Directors Disqualification Act 1986 and may be applied to an individual in the following circumstances:

(a) when convicted of an indictable offence in connection with the promotion, formation, management or liquidation of a company or the receivership or management of a company's property (s.2);

(b) when persistently in default in making returns. Three or more defaults in five years is conclusive proof (s.3);

(c) when guilty of fraudulent trading, fraud in relation to the company or breach of trust (s.4);

(d) when convicted three times in five years for offences in connection with company legislation (s.5);

(e) when the conduct of a person who was a Director of a company which has become insolvent makes him/her unfit to be a Director of a company (s.6);

(f) when following an Inspector's Report it seems expedient in the public interest (s.8);

(g) when a person through wrongful trading is liable to contribute to a company's assets (s.10).

These powers for the Court to disqualify a person from being a Director are optional except in the case of s.6 where if it is proved that the conduct of a former Director of an insolvent company makes him/her unfit to hold office he/she must be disqualified.

7:14 Insolvency Act 1986 – fraudulent and wrongful trading

Under the Insolvency Act 1986 the Directors can be made responsible for an insolvent company's debts and be personally liable to contribute towards the assets available for the satisfaction of creditors if they are found guilty of fraudulent or wrongful trading. They can also be prevented from using an insolvent company's name or acquiring its assets during a period from 12 months prior to going into liquidation to five years after the conclusion of the liquidation.

7:14.1 Fraudulent trading

Whilst most people have their own ideas of what constitutes fraudulent trading by a company the legal definition is more difficult. To be successful, a charge must show that the Director wilfully intended to defraud and in consequence the provisions have been little used. This led to the introduction in the Insolvency Act 1986 of the concept of wrongful trading.

7:14.2 Wrongful trading

Under these provisions a person can be required to contribute towards the assets of a company where:

(a)   that person was a Director or a Shadow Director of the company;

(b)   the company has gone into insolvent liquidation;

(c)   some time before the company went into liquidation that person knew, or should have known, that there was no reasonable prospect of avoiding insolvent liquidation.

The standard defence to such a charge is that the person concerned took all possible measures to minimise the loss to creditors as soon as it became obvious that there was no reasonable prospect of avoiding insolvent liquidation.

The responsibility for wrongful trading lies with all the Directors and a Director cannot plead ignorance of the financial position of the company. It is a Director's duty to ensure that he/she obtains sufficient advice for him/her to appreciate and understand the company's financial predicament.

Should a Director resign he/she still could be liable to contribute to the assets of the company in respect of the period up until his/her resignation.

7:14.3   Difficulty of determining time to stop trading

Should a major disaster befall the company or should some significant financial occurrence take place it may be relatively easy to see when a company has no reasonable prospect of avoiding insolvent liquidation. Should the company steadily decline through a period of ever worsening cash flow it becomes virtually impossible to determine the exact point of time when the company reaches a position of no recovery.

To stop trading too early could give rise to a charge from shareholders of breach of duty, removing from them the chance of recovery and stopping trading too late could give rise to a charge of wrongful trading.

7:14.4   Need for comprehensive records

However, a liquidator with the benefit of hindsight may find it far easier to estimate the time when the company ceased to have any reasonable prospects of avoiding insolvent liquidation.

It is therefore recommended that, should the company be approaching this position, extensive notes be kept of the information available to the Directors and the advice given to them by their financial and legal advisors that led them to believe that the company could be salvaged. Such information may well save the Directors from charges of wrongful trading or at least mitigate any demands made on them.

■ CHECK LIST ■

Who are the Directors of the company? ☐

Do any senior members of the staff have Director
in their title whilst not members of the Board? ☐

Does the company have any Shadow Directors? ☐

Are all appointments of Directors correctly minuted? ☐

Is retirement of Directors by rotation in accordance
with the Articles? ☐

Does the age limit for Directors apply and is a check
kept on the ages of the members of the Board? ☐

Is there a provision in the Articles to allow the
Board to remove one of their number? ☐

Are non-executive Directors kept fully informed
of events taking place within the company? ☐

Does the company have a procedure to record
Directors' outside interests? ☐

If the company is a Single Member Company and
the sole member is a Director are all contracts
outside normal business recorded? ☐

Are there any loans to Directors and is it certain
that they come within the permitted exceptions? ☐

Does the company carry Directors' and Officers'
Liability Insurance and was the contract entered
into by a disinterested quorum of the board? ☐

Are all Directors kept fully apprised of the
company's financial position? ☐

The Company Secretary

■ CHAPTER EIGHT ■

Contents

■ KEY QUESTIONS ■

Must the company have a Secretary?

Does the Company Secretary have to be qualified?

Is the Company Secretary regarded in law as an Officer of the company?

What are the routine duties of the Company Secretary?

What are the statutory liabilities of the Company Secretary?.

Where should the appointment of a Company Secretary be recorded?

Can the Company Secretary commit the company on contracts?

Can the Company Secretary be indemnified by the company?

8:1 The position of Company Secretary

In s.283 it states that every company must have a Secretary and where the company has a sole Director that person cannot also be Secretary. In s.284 it goes on to say that where anything is required to be done by a Director and the Secretary it cannot be satisfied by one person acting in two capacities. There must, therefore, be at least two persons involved in the management of a company.

8:2 Qualification of Company Secretary

In s.286 there is a requirement for the Secretary of a public company to be qualified. The qualifications mentioned as making a person suitable for appointment as Secretary of a public company are barrister, solicitor, member of the Institute of Chartered Secretaries and Administrators, the Institute of Chartered Accountants of England and Wales, Scotland or Ireland, the Association of Chartered Certified Accountants, the Institute of Cost and Management Accountants and the Chartered Institute of Public Finance and Accountancy. The Act does, however, allow the Directors to appoint a person not holding one of these qualifications who otherwise has the requisite experience to undertake the duties involved.

8:3 Secretary as Officer of the company

Legislation often refers to Officers of a company and s.744 defines an Officer as a Director, Manager or Secretary. This term Officer could, therefore, in certain circumstances encompass other senior personnel in the company but will always apply to the Secretary and as such he/she could be liable for any penalties specified for breaches of legislation.

8:4 Routine duties of the Company Secretary

The routine duties of a Company Secretary would normally encompass the following matters:

(a) ensuring compliance with the Companies Acts and the company's Memorandum and Articles of Association;

(b) for a publicly quoted company ensuring compliance with the Stock Exchange regulations (The Listing Rules otherwise known as the 'Yellow Book') and monitoring movements on the share register;

(c) maintaining or taking responsibility for the maintenance of the various statutory books;

(d) filing or taking responsibility for the filing of the various statutory returns required by Companies House and for the information required from publicly quoted companies by the Stock Exchange;

(e) where changes are required to the Memorandum, the Articles of Association or the authorised share capital ensuring that the documents are correctly drafted, the formalities of calling the meeting and passing the resolution are adhered to and the necessary returns are made to Companies House;

(f) ensuring that share certificates are properly issued to subscribers for the company's shares and that share transfers are correctly handled;

(g) calling and arranging meetings of the Directors and general meetings of the shareholders as directed by the Board and ensuring that notices of the meetings are correctly served;

(h) ensuring that copies of the Report and Accounts are dispatched to all persons entitled to receive them and that they are filed with the Registrar inside the stipulated time limits;

(i) preparing minutes of both Board Meetings and general meetings of members and maintaining those minute books and ensuring that they are kept secure and free from unauthorised access;

(j) ensuring that the statutory books are available for inspection and that where provided demands for copies can be met;

(k) ensuring that the seal is only used when properly authorised and that at other times it is kept secure and free from unauthorised access;

(l) acting as a liaison between the shareholders and the Directors as required.

The Company Secretary will also often be asked to give advice to the Directors and members of the staff on legislation and how it affects the company and the extent of this duty will depend on the experience and training of the Company Secretary and the other experienced staff employed by the company.

8:4.1   Statutory liabilities

The Company Secretary is also specifically charged under various statutes to ensure compliance with those statutes by the company and could incur personal liability if they are breached. The extent of the Company Secretary's duties in this respect depends upon the nature of the company's business and the other personnel employed by the company.

8:4.2   Other duties

The other duties undertaken by the Company Secretary will depend upon the nature of the company's business, the size of the undertaking and the other staff employed by the company. They will often encompass accountancy, personnel administration, insurances, pensions, data protection, share schemes and property administration. In a small company it is probable that all of these items will form part of the function of the Company Secretary.

8:5   Appointment

The appointment of the Company Secretary is within the power of the Board and the appointment to, resignation or the dismissal from, that position should be recorded in the appropriate Board Minutes. It is not considered necessary for the full terms of the appointment to be contained in the Board Minutes as the Secretary is an employee of the company, albeit a senior one, and details of the appointment should be contained in the personnel records.

8:6   Authority to commit the company

The extent to which the Company Secretary can commit the company should be recorded. If he/she is a signatory on the Bank mandate a resolution in the standard form required by the Bank will need to be passed. It is quite in order for the Secretary to commit the company on contracts especially where these are in accordance with decisions taken by the Directors, but the Secretary's authority should be minuted. Unless there are specific provisions to the contrary, it may be assumed that the Secretary does have the authority to commit the company in respect of routine administrative matters conducive to the efficient running of the company. [*Panorama Developments (Guildford) Ltd* v. *Fidelis Furnishing Fabrics Ltd.* (1971).]

8:7 Indemnity

As with the Directors, under s.310 the Secretary cannot be indemnified by the company for negligence, default, breach of duty or breach of trust except in defending proceedings, criminal or civil, where judgment is given in his/her favour or he/she is acquitted. It is permissible to take out insurance (Directors' and Officers' Liability Insurance) to cover these liabilities and where the company does take this insurance it no longer needs to be mentioned in the Annual Report.

8:8 Relationship with Directors

The relationship between the Company Secretary and the Chairman and the other Directors is a very important and unique one. It will, of course, depend on the personalities involved but a good working relationship must be to the advantage of the company and the Secretary needs to have easy access to the Chairman and/or Chief Executive. In a large company the Secretary will generally be regarded just as a senior member of the staff but in a smaller company will generally be a member of the management team. Whatever the size of the company the Company Secretary needs to be discreet, objective and knowledgeable about his/her subject.

■ CHECK LIST ■

Does the company have a Company Secretary? ☐

Is the Company Secretary (if the company is a public company) qualified? ☐

Is the Company Secretary considered an Officer of the company? ☐

Is the Company Secretary responsible for ensuring compliance by the company with all aspects of company legislation? ☐

Is the Company Secretary aware of other statutory liabilities laid upon him/her? ☐

Has the appointment been recorded in the Directors' minutes? ☐

Has the authority of the Company Secretary to commit the company been agreed and recorded? ☐

Is the Company Secretary covered by Directors' and Officers' Liability Insurance? ☐

Auditors

■ CHAPTER NINE ■

Contents

■ KEY QUESTIONS ■

Does a company have to have Auditors?

When must Auditors be appointed and who appoints them?

Can Auditors be appointed to continue in office from year to year?

What happens if the company fails to appoint Auditors?

Can the Directors fill a casual vacancy in the office of Auditor?

What information has to be given to Auditors?

Does the company have to notify Auditors of general meetings?

Can Auditors attend general meetings and speak at those meetings?

How are fees for Auditors fixed and do they have to be shown separately in the Accounts?

Can the company remove an Auditor from office?

What rights do Auditors have on leaving office to bring matters to the attention of members?

If Auditors are not reappointed each year as an elective resolution is in place, can the members seek their removal?

When an Auditor leaves office does he have to report to the members?

9:1   Need for Auditors

At times sight is lost of the reason that Auditors are required for companies. They are there to report to the shareholders on the stewardship of their company by the Directors. By s.384 (s.119, CA 1989) every company must have in place an Auditor unless it is a dormant company which has resolved not to make an appointment, or is a small company which is taking advantage of the audit exemption rules.

9:2   Appointment of Auditors

By s.385 (s.119, CA 1989) every public company and every private company which has not elected to dispense with laying Accounts before a general meeting must at each general meeting at which Accounts are laid, appoint Auditors to hold office from the conclusion of that meeting until the conclusion of the next general meeting at which Accounts are laid. The first Auditors may be appointed by the Directors at any time before the first Accounts are laid before a general meeting or by the members in general meeting if the Directors fail to make an appointment.

By s.385A (s.119, CA 1989) where a private company has passed an elective resolution not to lay Accounts before a general meeting but has not also passed an elective resolution not to appoint Auditors annually, the Auditors shall be appointed in a general meeting before the end of 28 days after the Accounts were dispatched or before the end of the meeting at which Accounts are considered if one is subsequently demanded.

By s.388A (The Companies Act 1985 (Audit Exemption) Regulations 1994 – SI 1994 No. 1935) a company which is dormant or is taking advantage of the audit exemption rules need not appoint Auditors. If, however, it is realised that the accounts are required to be audited the Directors may appoint Auditors at any time before those accounts are laid. The Auditors will hold office until the conclusion of the meeting at which those accounts are laid.

9:3 Elective resolution not to appoint Auditors annually

Where a private company has passed an elective resolution in accordance with s.386 (s.119, CA 1989) not to appoint Auditors annually the Auditors are deemed reappointed for each succeeding year until they resign or their appointment is terminated by a dormant company or small company eligible for audit exemption resolving not to appoint Auditors or a resolution is passed that their appointment be terminated.

9:4 Procedure if company fails to appoint Auditors

By s.387 (s.119, CA 1989), if Auditors are not appointed within the appropriate time limits the Secretary of State may make an appointment to fill the vacancy. Within one week of the end of the time for appointing Auditors if no appointment has been made then the company must advise the Secretary of State that his power is exercisable. Failure to give the requisite notice renders the company and every Officer in default liable to penalties.

9:5 Filling casual vacancy in the position

Under s.388 (s.119, CA 1989) the Directors have a power to fill a casual vacancy in the position of Auditor. At a general meeting of members special notice is required to fill a casual vacancy or to reappoint an Auditor appointed by the Directors to fill a casual vacancy. The resolution to appoint or reappoint the Auditors is an ordinary resolution but special notice has to be given to the company by a member 28 days prior to the meeting stating that the Auditors to be appointed are not those appointed the previous year now seeking reappointment.

Upon receipt of the special notice the company must forthwith send a copy to the person to be appointed and if the casual vacancy was caused by the resignation of an Auditor then a copy to that person as well.

9:6   Auditors' rights in office

The Auditors have the rights set out below and the sections quoted have been inserted into the Companies Act 1985 by s.120 of the Companies Act 1989:

(a)   a right of access at all times to the company's books, Accounts and vouchers and to obtain information and explanations from the company's Officers. An Officer of the company who knowingly or recklessly gives misleading, false or deceptive information is liable to a fine or imprisonment or both (s.389A);

(b)   to receive a copy of all notices of general meetings of the company (s.390);

(c)   to attend any general meeting of the company (s.390);

(d)   to be heard at any general meeting of the company on any matter which concerns them as Auditors (s.390);

(e)   to receive a copy of any written resolution proposed by a private company or otherwise be notified of its contents (s.381B as amended by SI 1996 No.1471).

9:7   Auditors' fees

The regulations state that the company shall determine in general meeting the fee to be paid to the Auditors. This impracticable position is generally resolved by the meeting delegating its responsibilities in this matter to the Directors who will agree the fee to be paid in a normal commercial manner.

The agreed sum together with any expenses incurred must be shown in the company's Annual Accounts (s.390A (s.121, CA 1989)). Regulations made under s.390B (s.121, CA 1989) now require companies to disclose by way of a note to their Accounts the total of all other sums paid to their Auditors for services other than auditing. These regulations do not apply to companies which come within the definition of a small or medium-sized company as set out in the Act (*see* **Para. 3:9.1**).

9:8 Replacement of Auditors

There are several regulations framed to preserve the independence of Auditors which do not allow the Directors to dispense with the current Auditors if their report is likely to be critical of the Directors' conduct of the company's affairs.

9:8.1 Removal of Auditor

A company may remove an Auditor from office by an ordinary resolution, of which special notice has been given, passed at a general meeting of the members. Within 14 days of passing the resolution the company must give notice to the Registrar on Form 391. The removed Auditor has the right to attend and be heard at a general meeting of the company up until the normal time of his/her retirement or when the appointment of his/her replacement is made (s.391 (s.122, CA 1989)).

Special notice as described above in connection with the appointment of an Auditor has to be given to remove an Auditor or to appoint a person other than the retiring Auditor. A copy of the notice has to be sent forthwith to the person proposed to be removed or to the retiring Auditor and to the person proposed to be appointed. The departing Auditor may request that a statement be sent to all members subject to safeguards to prevent undue publicity being given to defamatory material (s.391A (s.122, CA 1989)).

9:8.2 Resignation of Auditor

An Auditor might resign by notice in writing to the Registered Office of the company but it is not effective unless accompanied by the statement required by s.394 (see below). Within 14 days the company must send a copy of the notice of resignation to the Registrar (s.392 (s.122, CA 1989)).

9:8.3 Auditors' rights on resignation

When an Auditor resigns and believes there are circumstances which should be brought to the attention of the members and creditors he/she may require the Directors to call an Extraordinary General Meeting to consider those circumstances. The Directors must within 21 days convene the meeting to be held within a further 28 days.

The Auditor may also require a statement of reasonable length to be circulated to members subject to safeguards against undue publicity being given to defamatory matter (s.392A (s.122, CA 1989)).

It is difficult to see that this section will have much effect not least due to the fact that there is no provision for any resolution to be put before a meeting called under this section. If a course of action is decided upon by the members attending the meeting it will be for a shareholder to initiate it as there is obviously no agreement between the Directors and the Auditor which led to the meeting being called in the first place.

9:9 Rights of members when elective resolution in force

When there is in force an election passed by elective resolution not to appoint the Auditors annually any member may request, but not more than once a year, that their appointment be brought to an end. Such a request must be in writing directed to the Registered Office.

The Directors must convene a meeting to be held within 28 days of the deposit of the notice and if it is agreed that the Auditors appointment be brought to an end they will be deemed not to have been reappointed for the next financial year. If notice is given within 14 days of the circulation of the Accounts and it is agreed that their appointment be brought to an end then it will cease with that financial year.

If the Directors fail to call the meeting within 14 days then the requisitionist may call the meeting to be held within three months of the deposit of the notice (s.393 (s.122, CA 1989)).

9:10 Auditors' obligations upon leaving office

When an Auditor ceases to hold office for any reason he/she must deposit at the company's Registered Office a statement of any matters he/she believes should be brought to the attention of members and creditors or a statement that there are no such matters. If there are matters then within 14 days the company must send a copy to members or apply to the Court for the statement to be suppressed.

If application is made to the Court then the Auditor must be notified accordingly. Unless the Auditor is so notified within 21 days then within a further seven days he/she must send a copy of his/her statement to the Registrar.

If application is made to the Court then the Court will decide to suppress the statement or direct that it be circulated to the members (s.394 (s.123, CA 1989)). Where the Court suppresses a statement required by the Auditor to be circulated to the members, then that fact must be notified to all persons who would have been entitled to receive that statement.

Where an Auditor is resigning for normal commercial reasons it is important that a statement under s.394 is received from him/her stating that there are no matters to be brought to the attention of the members.

■ CHECK LIST ■

Are Auditors appointed each year when
Accounts are laid? ☐

If Accounts are not laid because an elective
resolution has been passed to dispense with
laying Accounts, are Auditors still appointed? ☐

Does an elective resolution need to be passed so that
Auditors remain in office from year to year? ☐

To avoid the Secretary of State making the appointment,
have the Auditors been appointed within the due time? ☐

Are the Directors aware that they have the power to fill a
casual vacancy in the office of Auditor? ☐

Do the Auditors have access to full and accurate
information at all times? ☐

Have the Auditors been informed of general meetings so that
they may attend and speak at the meetings if the matters
discussed affect them as Auditors? ☐

Have the Auditors' fees been agreed in general meeting
and have they been disclosed in the Accounts? ☐

Is the company aware that it may, in general meeting, remove
the Auditors prior to the expiry of their term of office? ☐

If the Auditors resign prior to the expiry of their
term of office have they advised members of any
matters which they believe should be brought
to their notice? ☐

Are members aware that when an elective resolution is in force
to provide for the automatic reappointment of Auditors
any member may seek their removal from office? ☐

Have the Auditors provided a statement of
satisfaction or otherwise upon leaving office? ☐

■ CHAPTER TEN ■

Calling a meeting

■ CHAPTER TEN ■

Contents

■ KEY QUESTIONS ■

For what purposes is a general meeting required?

Does the company have to hold an Annual General Meeting?

Can the company call any other general meetings apart from the Annual General Meeting?

Can the members demand an Extraordinary General Meeting and what happens if the Directors do not comply?

What must be stated in the notice of a meeting?

Can a member appoint a proxy to attend a meeting in his place?

How much notice has to be given of a meeting?

Can the members agree to short notice of a meeting?

What business has to be conducted at an Annual General Meeting?

Can the members add to that agenda?

Can the members also request comments to be circulated on resolutions proposed by the Directors?

When is special notice of an ordinary resolution required?

Can the company dispense with the Annual General Meeting by passing an elective resolution?

10:1   Need for General Meetings

The Directors are empowered to run the company in the manner in which they see fit and may take the necessary decisions to achieve the company's objectives. For certain actions, though, the Act states that the decision may not be that of the Directors alone and they have to submit the matter for the approval of the members at a general meeting or have it approved by the members in writing where applicable. The main items of business which must be approved by the members will include the following:

- **The business of the Annual General Meeting**
- **To alter the Memorandum or the Articles**
- **To grant the authority to the Directors to allot shares**
- **To set aside pre-emption rights**
- **To buy in the company's own shares**
- **To elect a Director as an alternative to that person being co-opted to the Board**
- **To remove a Director from office**
- **To remove the Auditors from office**
- **To ratify an *ultra vires* act undertaken by the Directors and to absolve the Directors from any liability from having acted *ultra vires***
- **To approve a contract in excess of £100,000 where a Director or Shadow Director is personally interested in that contract.**

There may be other items which could arise which would entail approval by the members and not solely by the Directors especially where the Stock Exchange Listing Rules are applicable.

10:2   Annual General Meeting

Each year every company, unless it is a private company which has passed an elective resolution not to hold Annual General Meetings, must hold an Annual General Meeting which must be described as such in the notice of the meeting and in the minutes. It must be held within 15 months of the previous year's Annual General Meeting (s.366).

For a newly incorporated company an Annual General Meeting need not be held in the year of incorporation or the following year provided the first Annual General Meeting is held within 18 months of incorporation.

10:3   Extraordinary General Meeting

Any other general meeting of members of the company is an Extraordinary General Meeting and is usually called by the Directors. Shareholders holding at least ten per cent of the voting rights may, however, require the Directors to call a meeting by depositing a written notice or notices at the Registered Office of the company, signed by the requisitionists and stating the objects of the meeting.

The Directors must convene a meeting within 21 days (s.368) to be held within a further 28 days (s.368(8) (Sch. 19, s.9, CA 1989)). If the Directors fail to convene a meeting within these time limits then the requisitionists or a number of them representing at least half of their voting rights may convene the meeting themselves to be held within three months of the expiration of the time limit for the Directors to convene the meeting.

If the requisitionists call the meeting themselves they may reclaim reimbursement from the company of reasonable expenses incurred, and such sums will be recovered by the company from any monies due to the Directors who were at fault in not calling the meeting.

10:4   Form of notice

The notice of the meeting must state the time and place where it is to be held and whether it is the Annual General Meeting or an Extraordinary General Meeting. It must also state the business to be conducted.

In the case of an Extraordinary General Meeting, the exact wording of the resolution(s) must be printed stating whether they are to be proposed as special, extraordinary, ordinary or elective resolutions as determined by the relevant section of the Act under which they are being enacted.

For an Annual General Meeting, the notice will state the routine business to be undertaken at that meeting together with the exact wording of any resolutions outside the routine business which are to be proposed. It must also be stated whether any such resolutions are to be proposed as special, extraordinary, ordinary or elective resolutions.

10:5   Proxies

The notice of all general meetings of a company with a share capital must also include a statement with reasonable prominence that a member may appoint a proxy to attend and vote in their place and that the proxy need not be a member of the company. Any requirement for proxy forms to be lodged with the company more than 48 hours before the relevant meeting is invalid.

If the company sends out unsolicited and at its own expense proxy forms naming a person or persons willing to act as a proxy they must be sent to all persons receiving notice and not just to some. This does not prevent a company from providing a proxy form in answer to a specific request where otherwise they are not being supplied.

10:6   Types of Resolution

The type of resolution to be used for any particular action will depend upon the requirements of the Act in the section under which the changes are being made. If the Act states that a resolution passed by the members in general meeting is required this means that an ordinary resolution will suffice. If any other type of resolution is required, e.g. a special resolution, this will be specified. The type of resolution which is being proposed must be set out in the notice of the meeting.

An ordinary resolution is one for which the notice set out in the next section has been given and it has been passed by a simple majority of those members voting.

A special or an extraordinary resolution is one for which the notice set out in the next section has been given and it has been passed by a 75% majority of those members voting. In this connection a 75% majority means that 75% of the members voting voted in favour. Only those members actually voting need to be considered, it is not that percentage of the total membership eligible to vote.

An elective resolution is one for which the notice set out in the next section has been given and which has been passed by everyone entitled to attend and vote. Approval may be given by members voting in person or by proxy or it may be passed in writing, but everyone entitled to vote must vote in favour.

10:7   Length of notice to be given

The length of notice required for a general meeting is determined by the business to be conducted at the meeting and is as set out below (s.369):

- **Annual General Meeting – 21 days**

- **Meeting to pass a special resolution which requires a 75 per cent majority – 21 days**

- **Meeting to pass an extraordinary resolution which requires a 75 per cent majority – 14 days**

- **Meeting to pass an ordinary resolution which requires a 50 per cent majority – 14 days**

- **Meeting of an unlimited company to pass an ordinary resolution which requires a 50 per cent majority – 7 days**

- **Meeting to pass an elective resolution which requires everyone entitled to attend and vote to approve either in person or by proxy – 21 days**

- **Meeting to pass an ordinary resolution of which special notice has been given – 21 days.**

Notice is deemed to have been served 48 hours after posting by first class mail unless the Articles provide otherwise. Notice is clear days notice and excludes the day of service and the day of the meeting for companies registered in England and Wales, but may include the day of the meeting for companies registered in Scotland. This difference comes from the differing decisions in two court cases. In an English case *re Hector Whaling Ltd (1936)* it was decided that the day of meeting could not be a day of notice. In a later Scottish case *Neil McLeod & Sons Ltd, Petitioners (1967)* it was decided that the last day of notice could be the day of the meeting.

Thus, notice which is posted by first class mail on day one is deemed served on day three, the first day of notice to count is day four, the last day of notice to count for a special resolution is day 24 and for a Scottish company this is the first day on which the meeting may be held. For a company registered in England or Wales the first day on which the meeting may be held is day 25. Weekends and Bank Holidays count as days of notice but, of course, may not count in calculating the day of receipt of notice by first class mail.

10:8   Short notice

Short notice of meetings is permissible if approved by the requisite majorities set out below:

- **Annual General Meeting – everyone entitled to attend and vote.**

- **Extraordinary General Meeting – holders of 95 per cent of the voting rights entitled to attend and vote. This percentage may, however, be reduced to 90 per cent for a private company which passes an elective resolution.**

- **Meeting to pass an elective resolution – everyone entitled to attend and vote.**

There would appear to be no provision for short notice of a meeting at which a resolution of which special notice has been given is to be considered.

10:9   Routine business of Annual General Meeting

The normal business of an Annual General Meeting is:

- **To receive the Annual Report and Accounts.**
- **To declare a dividend.**
- **To elect Directors.**
- **To appoint Auditors and to fix their remuneration.**

A private company may by passing an elective resolution dispense with the need to lay its Report and Accounts before a general meeting and dispense with the need to appoint its Auditors annually.

10:10   Members' rights regarding business of Annual General Meeting

The Directors may add any resolutions which they require to the basic agenda of the Annual General Meeting, but also members may require a resolution to be placed before the next Annual General Meeting. Similarly, members may require a statement not exceeding 1,000 words to be circulated to all members prior to any general meeting. In both of these cases requisitions must be in writing signed by holders of at least five per cent of the voting rights or by not less than 100 members holding on average £100 capital each, and be deposited at the Registered Office.

In the case of a resolution it must be deposited not less than six weeks before the Annual General Meeting and in the case of a statement not less than one week before the meeting. If an Annual General Meeting is called for less than six weeks after the deposit of a resolution the company must still comply with the request. The company or any aggrieved person may apply to the Court to prevent circulation of any statement where undue publicity is being given to defamatory matter (s.376).

10:11   Special notice

In certain cases special notice is required in connection with an ordinary resolution to be placed before a general meeting. By s.379 special notice has to be given by a member to the company in writing and deposited at the Registered Office not less than 28 days before the meeting, and the company has to give notice of such resolutions at the same time that it gives notice of the meeting to the members. If the meeting is called for a date less than 28 days after the notice has been deposited it will be deemed to have been validly given and the company must comply. The company must give 21 days notice of a meeting at which a resolution of which special notice has been given is going to be proposed and there would appear to be no provision for short notice.

Special notice is required for the following purposes:

- **To appoint Auditors other than those retiring, to remove Auditors or to re-appoint Auditors appointed by the Directors to fill a casual vacancy.**

- **To remove a Director prior to the expiry of his/her term of office.**

- **To appoint or reappoint a Director aged over 70 to the Board of a public company or a subsidiary of a public company.**

10:12 Elective resolution to dispense with Annual General Meeting

By s.366A (s.115(2), CA 1989) a private company may pass an elective resolution to dispense with the holding of Annual General Meetings. The resolution is effective for the year in which it is passed and for subsequent years.

Whilst the election is in force any member may require the company to hold an Annual General Meeting in any year by giving notice to the company in writing at its Registered Office not less than three months before the end of the year. If the election ceases to have effect the company need not hold an Annual General Meeting that year if there is less than three months of the year remaining.

■ CHECK LIST ■

Is an Annual General Meeting held every year? ☐

Is an Extraordinary General Meeting held when required by the Directors or when demanded by the members? ☐

Does the notice of the meeting state the business to be conducted? ☐

Does the notice of the meeting state that a member may appoint a proxy? ☐

Is the length of notice correct for the type of resolution to be passed at the meeting? ☐

Has short notice been agreed by the requisite percentage of members? ☐

Is all routine business to be conducted at the Annual General Meeting? ☐

Have Directors and members been allowed to add items to that agenda? ☐

Do the circumstances require that special notice of an ordinary resolution is given? ☐

Has the company passed an elective resolution to dispense with holding an Annual General Meeting? ☐

Conduct of a meeting

■ CHAPTER ELEVEN ■

Contents

■ KEY QUESTIONS ■

Where are the provisions covering the conduct of a meeting?

What are the duties of a Chairman in connection with a meeting?

What happens if a quorum is not present?

Can a member appoint a proxy?

Who acts as Chairman?

Who proposes the resolutions?

Can a member speak on any resolution?

Who can vote on a show of hands?

Who can vote on a poll?

Who can demand a poll?

When is a poll taken?

What preparations should be made if a poll is likely?

Do the members have to approve the Annual Report and Accounts at the Annual General Meeting?

What dividends have to be approved at the Annual General Meeting?

Do all Directors have to retire by rotation?

Do Auditors always have to be re-elected at the Annual General Meeting?

Who fixes the Auditors' remuneration?

11:1 Chairman's duties in running a meeting

Once a meeting has been called it must be conducted not only in accordance with the provisions of the Companies Acts but also in accordance with the company's Articles. Within these parameters it is for the Chairman to conduct the meeting how he/she sees fit.

The Chairman must ensure that all shades of opinion have their opportunity to state their case, that a vote is properly taken and that his/her declaration of the result of that vote correctly reflects the decision of the meeting.

If the Chairman has a casting vote, which must be provided for in the Articles, then he/she should use it with discretion in the best interests of the company. Normally, a Chairman would not use his/her casting vote to pass a resolution on the basis that if it did not command an outright majority without his/her support then the company has not shown the will to implement the changes proposed.

Unless the Articles make special provision to the contrary the Chairman may only adjourn a meeting with the permission of those present.

11:2 Quorum

When a meeting convenes the Secretary should ensure that only those persons entitled to attend and vote are in attendance. At the appointed time, if a quorum is present, the meeting should proceed to business. Unless otherwise stated in the Articles a quorum is two members personally present. Table A states that a quorum is two persons present in person or by proxy.

The procedure to be followed if a quorum is not present will depend upon the company's Articles, but Table A provides that if a quorum is not present within 30 minutes of the appointed time then the meeting is adjourned to the same time and place on the same day of the following week or some such other time as determined by the Directors.

By s.370A (The Companies (Single Member Private Limited Companies) Regulations 1992 – SI 1992 No. 1699) the quorum for a single member company is one person present in person or by proxy and this rule will override anything to the contrary in the company's Articles.

11:3   Proxies

Any member may appoint a proxy to attend a meeting in his/her place and that person need not be a member of the company. Articles generally provide in a private company that a proxy may speak at a meeting as well as vote, but in a public company the proxy may normally only vote. Unless the Articles provide otherwise, in a private company a member may only appoint one proxy for any one meeting and proxies normally may not vote on a show of hands but only vote on a poll or join in a demand for a poll. The actual rights of proxies will depend on the provisions contained in that company's Articles.

The duly appointed representative of a corporate shareholder is not a proxy but a member with all the rights of a member.

11:4   Who is Chairman?

The Chairman of the meeting will normally be the Chairman of the Board of Directors but again if the Articles make other provisions they should be followed. Table A provides that the Chairman of the Board will take the chair at any general meeting or in his absence then some other Director nominated by the Board.

If neither of these people is present within 15 minutes of the time set down for the start of the meeting then the Directors present shall appoint one of their number and if there is only one Director present he/she shall take the chair. If within 15 minutes of the appointed time for the commencement of the meeting there is no Director present or no Director willing to act as Chairman then the meeting shall choose one of the members present to be Chairman.

11:5   Procedure in the meeting

Once the meeting has commenced the resolutions which have been set down in the notice of the meeting shall be put to the meeting. They would be proposed and preferably seconded. If they were resolutions initiated by the Directors then normally the Chairman or one of the other Directors would propose the motion and give some background information and the Board's reasons for wishing to implement the measures.

If the resolution is one which has been put before the meeting following the appropriate requisition from members of the company then it will be proposed by one of the requisitionists who will speak on behalf of the resolution.

Once the motion has been put to the meeting it would be open for debate by the members present. When the Chairman is satisfied that the matter has been thoroughly discussed and that all shades of opinion have had an opportunity to state their point of view he should put the motion to a vote.

A resolution of which notice has been given to the members may not be amended at the meeting, only approved or rejected. If it is required that it be approved in an amended form fresh notice of the amended resolution would have to be given to the members and a further meeting held. It is normally permissible to amend a resolution at a meeting to correct minor errors or inaccurate drafting [*re Moorgate Mercantile Holdings Ltd (1980)*.]

11:6   Voting on a show of hands

Initially, voting is on a show of hands where every member has one vote and the Chairman's declaration of the result of that vote is conclusive proof without stating the actual numbers voting for or against the resolution.

11:7   Voting on a poll

Once the Chairman has declared the result of the voting then any member present or any proxy may demand that the proposal be put to a poll.

On a poll, members normally have one vote per share that they hold, though again the Articles may make some different provisions in this respect, but the voting will still be proportional to the individual shareholdings.

Whilst any member may demand or join in a demand for a poll the Articles may stipulate that such a demand must be supported by at least five members personally present or represented by a proxy or by holders of not less than ten per cent of the voting rights or some such lesser figures.

11:7.1   *When is the poll vote taken?*

The arrangements for a poll will depend upon the Articles and Table A provides that a poll shall be taken at the meeting itself or if this is not convenient at some other time or place as the Chairman decides or may be taken by post. If the date and time of the poll is not announced at the meeting itself then at least seven days' notice must be given to all members.

11:8   Arrangements for a poll

Where there is any likelihood of a poll being demanded then arrangements must be made to at least provide for the following items:

(a)   check the voting entitlement of all members;

(b)   check the validity of proxies;

(c)   have available additional copies of the resolution upon which voting is taking place;

(d)   have voting papers available;

(e)   have facilities to check that the votes have been validly cast;

(f)   have persons available to count the votes and to have that count independently verified if this is thought necessary.

The procedure outlined above would normally be followed as appropriate for an Extraordinary General Meeting or in respect of resolutions added to the normal business of an Annual General Meeting. Other considerations apply to the normal business of the Annual General Meeting.

11:9   Procedures for routine business of an Annual General Meeting

11:9.1   *Annual Report and Accounts*

Unless an elective resolution has been passed not to lay the Annual Report and Accounts before the company in general meeting these documents must be brought before a meeting which is normally the Annual General

Meeting. These documents do not have to be approved by the meeting, for the Directors' duty is merely to present them to that meeting.

In many companies it is the practice to take a vote on the Report and Accounts but this vote is of no consequence and if the shareholders were to vote against their acceptance it does not alter the fact that those Accounts are the accounts of the company and the Report is the report of the Directors. A vote against the Report and Accounts is tantamount to a vote of no confidence in the Board but has no legal effect.

11:9.2   Dividends

The provisions with regard to the proposal or approval of dividends are contained within the Articles and the provisions of Table A stated below are commonly used. The dividend which may be declared as part of the normal business of the Annual General Meeting is a final dividend for any financial period. The amount declared will normally be that recommended by the Directors but it may be less than that recommended but never more. Interim dividends declared by the Directors do not require approval by a general meeting of members, their declaration being within the power of the Directors.

11:9.3   Election of Directors

Directors retire by rotation and put themselves up for re-election only if it is provided for in the Articles. Without these provisions a Director once appointed stays in office until he/she retires or a resolution is passed to remove that Director from office. At the Annual General Meeting of a private company a combined resolution to reappoint a number of Directors is permissible but such a resolution may only be moved in a public company if previously a resolution authorising the re-election of the Directors in a combined resolution is passed with no-one voting against it.

11:9.4   Election of Auditors

At every meeting at which Accounts are laid, Auditors must be appointed to hold office until the conclusion of the next meeting at which Accounts are laid. These provisions may, however, be set aside by a private company which passes an elective resolution not to appoint Auditors annually whereby the Auditors stay in office until they resign, a resolution is moved to end their appointment or the company becomes dormant and passes a resolution to dispense with the appointment of Auditors, or it is a small company which takes advantage of the audit exemption rules.

Where Auditors are appointed in general meeting then the meeting must also fix their remuneration. For practical purposes, this normally results in the meeting delegating their responsibility to fix their remuneration to the Directors who will negotiate the audit fee with the Auditors. Although it is becoming much more common for companies to change Auditors to achieve cost savings, this does not relieve them of the liability to appoint Auditors at every meeting at which Accounts are laid and the detailed provisions covering a change of Auditor as set out in **Chapter 9** must be followed.

■ CHECK LIST ■

Does the Chairman conduct the meeting in accordance
with the regulations? ☐

Does the Chairman allow all shades of opinion to
be expressed and to obtain the majority view of
the meeting? ☐

Is a quorum always present? ☐

Are members allowed to appoint a proxy to attend and vote
in their place? ☐

Do the Articles designate who should chair the meeting? ☐

Are members given the opportunity to express their views
about resolutions that are put to the meeting before
the vote is taken? ☐

Is initial voting on a show of hands? ☐

Can a poll be demanded if members feel the result of the vote
does not reflect the majority view of the membership? ☐

Are members aware that the poll need not be taken at the
meeting? ☐

Are the arrangements for a poll carefully made? ☐

Are members aware that a vote is not required when the
Annual Report and Accounts are laid before the
Annual General Meeting? ☐

Are members aware that the dividend approved at the Annual
General Meeting is normally that recommended by the
Directors, it may not be increased? ☐

Are Directors only required to retire by rotation if provided
for in the Articles? ☐

Is an elective resolution in force allowing Auditors to remain
in office, thus dispensing with the need to be reappointed
annually? ☐

Written resolutions

■ **CHAPTER TWELVE** ■

Contents

■ KEY QUESTIONS ■

Do the regulations apply to all companies?

Who has to sign a written resolution?

Does the company have to advise the Auditors?

What records have to be kept of a written resolution?

Can the company use a written resolution even though the articles state that a meeting must be held?

Are there any resolutions for which a written resolution cannot be used?

12:1   Introduction

Section 113 of the Companies Act 1989 introduced into the Companies Act 1985, s.381A which allows any private company to pass a resolution in writing instead of putting it before a general meeting. A number of companies have a similar authority in their Articles and may continue to follow their Articles or the provisions in the Act according to which is most convenient for the company.

12:2   Signatures required

The regulations apply only to private companies and state that instead of passing a resolution at a meeting of members the company can have a copy or copies of that resolution signed by ALL MEMBERS entitled to attend and vote. The date of the resolution will be the date that the last person signed it.

12:3   Submission to Auditors

By s.381B (s.113, CA 1989 as amended by SI 1996 No 1471) a copy of every proposed written resolution must be sent to the Auditors or they must otherwise be notified of its contents. Notification must be at or before the time the resolution is first sent to a member for signature. Failure to notify the Auditors does not invalidate the resolution but does lay open to penalties both the Company Secretary and the Directors.

12:4   Minuting written resolutions

The signed copy or copies of the resolution should be entered into the minute book and when countersigned by the Secretary or a Director the written resolution is deemed to have complied with all the necessary regulations until the contrary is proved.

12:5   Overriding other provisions

The provisions for written resolutions in s.381A override any other regulations with regard to notice or specific majorities, but must have the signed acceptance of EVERY MEMBER of the company who is entitled to attend meetings and vote at such meetings.

12:6   Limitations on use

Under Sch. 15A inserted into the Companies Act 1985 by s.114 of the Companies Act 1989 it is provided that a written resolution may not be used to remove a Director prior to the expiry of his term of office or to remove an Auditor prior to the expiry of his term of office. Any such resolutions must be submitted to a general meeting of members.

In those cases where a resolution placed before a general meeting would need to have available for inspection by the members certain documents, then if passed in writing copies of those documents must be provided to the members with the proposed written resolution. Where a member stands to benefit from the passage of a resolution by the company, the votes of that member will be ignored in determining whether the resolution has been passed or not. Similar provisions apply should that resolution be passed in writing.

■ CHECK LIST ■

Are written resolutions signed by all members? ☐

Are written resolutions submitted to the Auditors? ☐

Are written resolutions entered in the minute book and countersigned by a Director or the Secretary? ☐

Are all members aware that these provisions override anything to the contrary in the Articles as to notice or specific majority? ☐

Are all members aware that a written resolution cannot be used to remove a Director or Auditor from office? ☐

Would special provisions apply if the resolution was put to a general meeting and have they been applied to a written resolution? ☐

Elective regime

Contents

■ KEY QUESTIONS ■

How does the company pass an elective resolution?

How does a company cancel an elective resolution?

Does the company have to notify the Registrar of any elective resolutions that have been passed?

What happens if the new regulations differ from the Articles?

For what purposes can an elective resolution be used?

How can the Annual General Meeting be completely cancelled?

13:1   Introduction

Section 116 of the Companies Act 1989 inserts into the Companies Act 1985, s.379A which gives effect to the elective regime whereby private companies may dispense with some of the administrative procedures set out in the Act.

13:2   Requirements of an elective resolution

In order to take advantage of these concessions the company must pass the appropriate elective resolution. The company must give 21 days' notice of a meeting at which an elective resolution is to be proposed and the notice must state the fact that the resolution will be proposed as an elective resolution.

To be effective the resolution must be agreed to by EVERY MEMBER entitled to attend the meeting and vote thereat either in person or by proxy. Alternatively, the resolution may be passed in writing for which the regulations also stipulate that it must be agreed to by everyone entitled to attend and vote.

13:3   Revoking elective resolutions

An elective resolution may be revoked by an ordinary resolution which only requires a 50 per cent majority. An elective resolution will automatically be revoked if a private company re-registers as a public company.

13:4   Filing with the Registrar

Copies of all elective resolutions and all resolutions revoking elective resolutions must be filed with the Registrar within 15 days of being passed by the company.

13:5   Elective resolutions override Articles

These regulations concerning elective resolutions override any provisions to the contrary in the company's Articles of Association.

13:6   Uses of elective resolutions

An elective resolution may be used for the following purposes:

(a)   to extend the period during which Directors may allot shares so that it may exceed five years (s.80A (s.115, CA 1989));

(b)   to dispense with the laying of Reports and Accounts before a general meeting (s.252 (s.16, CA 1989));

(c)   to dispense with the holding of an Annual General Meeting (s.366A (s.115, CA 1989));

(d)   to reduce the majority required to authorise short notice of a meeting, other than the Annual General Meeting, to less than 95 per cent provided that the figure is not less than 90 per cent (s.369(4) and s.378(3) (s.115, CA 1989));

(e)   to dispense with the appointment of Auditors annually (s.386 (s.119, CA 1989)).

13:7   Annual General Meeting

Whilst it was quite clearly the intention of the legislation for private companies to be able to dispense with the annual ritual of the Annual General Meeting (AGM) and the activities which took place at that meeting, the regulations are not comprehensive in this respect. There is no facility specified to cope with the reappointment of Directors retiring by rotation nor for the approval of a final dividend proposed by the Directors, both of which would normally be dealt with at the AGM.

If it is intended to dispense entirely with the activities associated with the Annual General Meeting then an alternative to a resolution passed at the AGM has to be found for these two items, and some suggestions are set out below.

13:7.1   Written resolutions

Firstly, written resolutions could be used to re-elect the Directors retiring by rotation and to approve the final dividend for the year. Whilst a written resolution cannot be used to remove a Director prior to the expiry of his term of office it can be used to re-elect a Director. Alternatively, the need for these two resolutions to be passed at all could be removed in the manner set out in the following two sections.

13:7.2   Non declaration of final dividend

It is only a final dividend that needs approval from the members in general meeting whereas an interim dividend is in the control of the Directors and does not require the approval of the members. It is suggested that instead of the Directors proposing a final dividend that they declare an interim or a second interim dividend.

13:7.3   Removal of retirement by rotation

With regard to the re-election of Directors, there is only a need for Directors to retire by rotation if it is stipulated in the Articles of Association.

Without such a provision Directors once appointed remain in office until they resign or a resolution is passed to remove them from office. If, therefore, it is desired to dispense with all the formalities of the Annual General Meeting then, if necessary, the Articles should be altered to remove the necessity for the Directors to retire by rotation.

■ CHECK LIST ■

Has an elective resolution been approved by all members? ☐

Have any ordinary resolutions been passed
revoking elective resolutions? ☐

Have copies of all elective resolutions and resolutions
revoking elective resolutions been filed with
the Registrar? ☐

Are members aware that these regulations override anything
to the contrary in the Articles? ☐

Are members aware that elective resolution can be used to:

(a) dispense with the Annual General Meeting? ☐

(b) dispense with laying the Annual Report and
Accounts? ☐

(c) dispense with appointing Auditors annually? ☐

(d) reduce the majority for short notice of a meeting? ☐

(e) extend the period in which the Directors may
allot shares? ☐

Are members aware that further measures are required to fully
dispose of the Annual General Meeting? ☐

Are members aware that the Annual General Meeting can be
disposed of by:

(a) use of written resolutions? or ☐

(b) declaring interim dividends instead of final
dividends? and ☐

(c) changing Articles to remove need for Directors
to retire by rotation? ☐

Change of company name

■ CHAPTER FOURTEEN ■

Contents

■ KEY QUESTIONS ■

What restrictions are there on the choice of company name?

Once registered can the company be forced to change its name?

How does a company proceed to change its name?

How is the new name registered with Companies House?

When is the Certificate of Change of Name issued?

When is the change effective?

What measures need to be taken to put the change into effect?

What also needs to be considered if the company is changing its trade?

How can a company keep a check whether another company is registered with a similar name?

Can a company dispense with using the word 'limited'?

Do you operate under a business name?

14:1 Introduction

When the Directors are of the opinion that a change of name would be beneficial to the company there are many factors which they must take into account.

14:2 Restrictions on the choice of name

The new name that they choose must not:

(a) include the word 'Limited' except as the last word of the name or as part of 'Public Limited Company'. The abbreviations 'Ltd', 'PLC' and 'plc' are acceptable;

(b) be the same as a name currently on the Register. In determining whether a name is the same, punctuation, articles, 'Co' and 'and Co' are ignored but '&' and 'and' are regarded as being the same;

(c) be one, the use of which would constitute a criminal offence. Various statutes limit the use of certain words to people or companies registered under those statutes as shown in the **Appendix** at the end of this Chapter;

(d) be one which is offensive. It is at the Secretary of State's discretion as to whether a name is offensive. It is unlikely, for example, that a name containing a swear word or implying an immoral purpose would be allowed to be registered;

(e) give the impression of connections with HM Government or any Local Authority, except with the permission of the Secretary of State;

(f) include any word or expression specified in regulations made under s.29, CA 1985 (*see* **Appendix** at the end of this Chapter).

Companies House will give advice as to whether a name is acceptable to them and this should be done if there is any question over their acceptance of the name desired. Companies House will not, however, reserve a name and the name desired has to be available at the time that the application to use it reaches Companies House.

Care should also be taken if it is at all possible that the name chosen may infringe any trade mark or other proprietary rights in the name.

14:3   Powers of DTI to enforce change of name

Care should be taken over the choice of name as the Department of Trade and Industry has the power in three circumstances to force a company to change its name. These circumstances are:

- **Where it is considered that a name is too like a name already on the Register. The order to the company to change its name must be made within 12 months of registration and the order will state the time scale in which the change must take place.**

- **Where the name is misleading as to the nature of the company's activities such that it could cause harm to the public. The change must take place within six weeks of being ordered unless the company within three weeks of the order applies to the Court to have it set aside.**

- **Where the company was allowed to use a name on production of misleading information or on giving undertakings which have not been kept. The change must be ordered within five years of registration and must take place within the time scale set down in the order.**

14:4   Effecting a change of name

A change of name has to be approved by special resolution passed by the members in general meeting, or in the case of a private company may be passed by the members by written resolution. The resolution may be passed at an Extraordinary General Meeting specially called for the purpose or added to the agenda of the Annual General Meeting and in all cases the actual wording of the resolution must be set out in the notice of the meeting. An example of such a resolution could be:

'The following resolution will be proposed as a special resolution: That the name of the company be changed to XYZ LTD.'

As it is not possible to reserve a particular name for a company to use it is always possible that someone else could adopt the name proposed during the period that the planning of the change is taking place. It is therefore essential that a check of the Register of Names at Companies House be made as late as possible before issuing to the members the notice of the meeting at which the resolution to change the name is to be proposed. The Register of Names may be accessed on the internet at http://www.companieshouse.gov.uk and is also available on fiche at most main public libraries, though these fiche are only updated once per quarter.

14:5 Registering change of name with Companies House

When the resolution has been passed it is necessary to prepare a certified copy for submission to the Registrar and this could be set out in the following form:

ABC LTD   Co. No.:XXXXXXXX

At a meeting of the company held on.........................199- at.........................the following resolution was passed as a special resolution.

THAT the name of the company be changed to XYZ LTD.

Signed............................
Chairman/Director/Secretary

Within 15 days of passing the resolution the copy resolution certified by a Director or the Secretary must be sent to the Registrar together with any permission granted by the relevant authority to use any specified word in the name of the company and a remittance for £10.

14:6 Issue of Certificate of Change of Name

The Registrar will issue a Certificate of Change of Name and it is at this point that the change becomes effective. As has been previously mentioned, it is not possible to reserve a name at Companies House so it is advisable to file the documents as soon as possible after the resolution has been passed, rather than using the 15 days allowed in the Act, to minimise the risk of the name being taken by someone else in the intervening period.

14:7 Effecting change within the company

Once the Certificate of Change of Name has been received the following items need to be carried out to effect the change:

(a)   attach a copy of the resolution to all copies of the Memorandum and Articles of Association, unless it is proposed to reprint these documents;

(b)   advise staff;

(c)   change letter headings, name boards, etc;

(d)   advise Bankers, Auditors, Solicitors and other professional advisors;

(e)   advise customers, suppliers and other trading connections;

(f)   advise the Inland Revenue, Customs and Excise, Contributions Agency, Rating Authority, Vehicle Licensing Authority and any other relevant statutory bodies.

14:7.1   Change of trade

If the change of name is accompanied by a change of trade then several other matters need to be borne in mind:

(a)   is the new trade one which is permitted by the Objects Clause of the Memorandum?

(b)   are there any loans made to the company by the Bank or from elsewhere which contain restrictions as to the trade to be followed by the company?

(c)   are there any planning restrictions which would prevent any alternative trade being carried out at the company's premises?

(d)   will a change of trade adversely affect the company's tax position especially with regard to the availability of tax losses to be carried forward?

14:8   Name watching service

If a company's name is particularly valuable and a considerable amount of goodwill is attached to it the company will probably wish to protect that name and ensure that no-one registers a name which could be confused with it. As has been seen, Companies House will register a name if it is not the same as a name already on the Register even though it may be very similar. Should such circumstances arise, the company may well wish to request that the Department of Trade force the new company to change its name and such a change must be made within one year of registration. To keep a watch on such a situation developing it is usual to employ one of the organisations offering a name watching service to monitor any names registered which may be confused with the name of your company.

14:9   Dispensing with the word 'limited'

In certain circumstances as set out in s.30 a company may dispense with using the word 'limited' in its name. To qualify for this concession the company must:

(a)   be a private company limited by guarantee;

(b)   have as its Objects the promotion of commerce, art, science, education, religion, charity or any profession.

The Memorandum or Articles of Association must also state that:

(a)   any profits or other income must be applied in promoting the Objects of the company;

(b)   no dividends may be paid to members;

(c)   in the event of a winding-up any surplus assets otherwise available to the members be transferred to another body with similar objects or to a charity.

To obtain the concession to omit 'limited' from the name:

(a)   in the case of a new company, submit with the documents of incorporation a statutory declaration on Form 30(5)(A) signed by a Solicitor engaged in the formation of the company or by a person named as a Director or the Secretary stating that all the necessary requirements have been met; or

(b)   in the case of an existing company, pass a special resolution to change the name and file with the other documents with the Registrar a statutory declaration on Form 30(5)(A) signed by a Director or by the Secretary that all the necessary requirements have been met.

14:10   Business names

It is open for anyone to trade in any name that they like subject to certain restrictions similar to those under Section 29 of the Companies Act 1985. Where, however, that trading name is not the full name of the proprietors of the business, whether it be a sole trader, partnership or corporate body, then compliance must be made with the Business Names Act 1985. In the case of a sole trader or partnership the full name of the proprietor(s) of the business may be the surname(s) with or without christian or fore names or initials.

Where compliance with Business Names Act 1985 is required there must be shown the name(s) of the proprietor(s) of the business together with the address where legal documents may be served upon them on all letterheads, invoices, receipts and written demands for the payment of debts. Similar information must also be displayed in all premises from which the business is conducted.

APPENDIX

Restricted words and expressions

Extract from 'Guidance Booklet GBF2—Company Names' published by the Department of Trade and Industry (Companies Registration Office).

You will need the approval of The Secretary of State for Trade and Industry before you use any of the following words or expressions (or their plural or possessive forms) in your chosen company name. More detailed information as to the circumstances in which certain words and expressions may be used in a company name is given in the Guidance Booklet mentioned above.

(a) Words which imply national or international pre-eminence:

British	International	Scottish
England	Ireland	United Kingdom
English	Irish	Wales
European	National	Welsh
Great Britain	Scotland	

(b) Words which imply business pre-eminence or representative or authoritative status:

Association	Council	Institution
Authority	Federation	Society
Board	Institute	

(c) Words which imply specific objects or functions:

Assurance	Chemistry	Reassurance
Assurer	Co-operative	Re-assurer
Benevolent	Foundation	Register
Chamber of	Friendly society	Registered
Commerce	Fund	Re-insurance
Chamber of	Group	Re-insurer
Commerce,	Holding	Sheffield
Training & Enterprise	Industrial &	Stock exchange
Chamber of Industry	provident society	Trade Union
Chamber of Trade	Insurance	Trust
Charter	Insurer	
Chartered	Patent	
Charity	Patentee	
Chemist	Post office	

Words or expressions in the following list need the approval of the Secretary of State. If you want to use any of them in your company name you will need to write first to the relevant body to ask whether they have any objection to its use. When you apply for approval to use the name, you should tell Companies House that you have written to the relevant body and enclose a copy of the reply you have received.

Word or expression	Relevant body for companies intending to have registered office in England or Wales	Relevant body for companies intending to have registered office in Scotland
Apothecary	The Worshipful Society of Apothecaries of London Apothecaries Hall Blackfriars Lane London EC4V 6EJ	The Royal Pharmaceutical Society of Great Britain Law Department 1 Lambeth High Street London SE1 7JN
Charity, charitable	Charity Commission Registration Division St. Alban's House 57-60 Haymarket London SW1Y 4QX *or* *for companies **not** intending to register as a charity* Charity Commission 2nd Floor 20 Kings Parade Queens Dock Liverpool L3 4DQ	*For recognition as a Scottish charity* Inland Revenue FICO (Scotland) Trinity Park House South Trinity Road Edinburgh EH5 3SD
Contact lens	The Registrar General Optical Council 41 Harley Street London W1N 2DJ	As for England and Wales
Dental, dentistry	The Registrar General Dental Council 37 Wimpole Street London W1M 8DQ	As for England and Wales
District nurse, health visitor, midwife, midwifery, nurse, nursing	The Registrar & Chief Executive United Kingdom Central Council for Nursing, Midwifery and Health Visiting 23 Portland Place London W1N 3JT	As for England and Wales

Word or expression	Relevant body for companies intending to have registered office in England or Wales	Relevant body for companies intending to have registered office in Scotland
Health centre	Office of the Solicitor Department of Health 48 Carey Street London WC2A 2LS	As for England and Wales
Health service	NHS Management Executive Department of Health Wellington House 135-155 Waterloo Road London SE1 8UG	As for England and Wales
Police	Home Office Police Dept Strategy Group Room 510 50 Queen Anne's Gate London SW1H 9AT	The Scottish Ministers Police Division St Andrew's House Regent Road Edinburgh EH1 3DG
Polytechnic	Department for Education and Science FHE 1B Sanctuary Buildings Great Smith Street Westminster London SW1P 3BT	As for England and Wales
Pregnancy, termination, abortion	Department of Health Area 423 Wellington House 133-135 Waterloo Road London SE1 8UG	As for England and Wales
Royal, royale, royalty, king, queen, prince, princess, Windsor, duke, His/Her Majesty	Home Office A Division Room 1378 50 Queen Anne's Gate London SW1H 9AT (if based in England) Welsh Office Crown Buildings Cathays Park Cardiff CF1 3NQ (if based in Wales)	The Scottish Ministers Civil Law & Legal Division Saughton House Broomhouse Drive Edinburgh EH11 3XD

Word or expression	Relevant body for companies intending to have registered office in England or Wales	Relevant body for companies intending to have registered office in Scotland
Special school	Department for Education and Employment Schools 2 Branch Sanctuary Buildings Great Smith Street Westminster London SW1P 3BT	As for England and Wales
University	Privy Council Office 68 Whitehall London SW1A 2AT	As for England and Wales

Certain words or expressions are covered by other legislation and their use in company names might be a criminal offence. These are listed below. If you want to use any of these words or expressions in your company name, then you should contact the relevant regulatory authority or ask Companies House for advice before proceeding. Companies House may seek independent advice from the relevant body.

Word or expression	Relevant legislation	Relevant body
Architect	s.20 Architects Registration Act 1997	Architects Registration Board 73 Hallam Street London W1N 6EE
Credit Union	Credit Union Act 1979	The Registrar of Friendly Societies 25 The North Colonnade Canary Wharf London E14 5HS
		For Scottish Registered Companies Assistant Registrar of Friendly Societies 58 Frederick Street Edinburgh EH2 1NB
Olympiad, Olympiads, Olympian, Olympians, Olympic, Olympics or translation of these	Olympic Symbol etc. (Protection) Act 1995*	British Olympic Association 1 Wandsworth Plain London SW18 1EH
	* Also protects Olympic symbol of five interlocking rings and motto 'Citius Altius Fortius'	

Word or expression	Relevant legislation	Relevant body
Veterinary surgeon, veterinary, vet	ss.19/20 Veterinary Surgeons Act 1966	The Registrar Royal College of Veterinary Surgeons 62–64 Horseferry Road London SW1P 2AF
Dentist, dental surgeon, dental practitioner	Dental Act 1984	The Registrar General Dental Council 37 Wimpole Street London W1M 8DQ
Drug, druggist, pharmaceutical, pharmaceutist, pharmacist, pharmacy	s.78 Medicines Act 1968	The Director of Legal Services The Royal Pharmaceutical Society of Great Britain 1 Lambeth High Street London SE1 7JN *For Scottish Registered Companies* The Pharmaceutical Society 36 York Place Edinburgh EH1 3HU
Optician, opthalmic optician, dispensing optician, enrolled optician, registered optician, optometrist	Opticians Act 1989	The Registrar General Optical Council 41 Harley Street London W1N 2DJ
Bank, Banker, Banking, Deposit	Banking Act 1987	Authorisation Enquiries Financial Services Authority 25 The Colonnade Canary Wharf London E14 5HS
Red Cross, Geneva Cross, Red Crescent, Red Lion and Sun	Geneva Convention Act 1957	Seek Advice of Companies House
Anzac	s.1 Anzac Act 1916	Seek Advice of Companies House
Insurance broker, Assurance broker, Re-insurance broker, Re-assurance broker	ss.2/3 Insurance Brokers (Registration) Act 1977	Seek Advice of The Insurance Brokers Council Higham Business Centre Midland Road Higham Ferrers Northants

Word or expression	Relevant legislation	Relevant body
Chiropodist, dietician, medical laboratory technician, occupational therapist, orthoptist, physiotherapist, radiographer remedial gymnast	Professions Supplementary to Medicine Act 1960 if preceded by Registered, State or Registered	Room 12.26 HAP4 Division Department of Health Hannibal House Elephant & Castle London SE1 6TE
Institute of Laryngology, Institute of Otology, Institute of Urology, Institute of Orthopaedics	University College London Act 1988	Seek advice of University College, London Gower Street London WC1E 6BT
Patent Office, Patent Agent	Copyright, Designs and Patents Act 1988	IPCD Hazlitt House 45 Southampton Buildings London WC2A 1AR
Building society	Building Society Act 1986	Seek advice of The Building Societies Commission Victoria House 30–34 Kingsway London WC2B 6ES

Crown Copyright. Reproduced with the permission of the Controller of Her Majesty's Stationery Office.

■ CHECK LIST ■

Is the name unique and does it contain restricted words? ☐

Is the Board aware that the company can be forced to change name if objections raised within 12 months of registration? ☐

Has a special resolution been passed to change name? ☐

Has the new name been registered with Companies House? ☐

Has the company received the Certificate of Change of Name? – the change only becomes effective upon issue of this certificate. ☐

Are copy resolutions being included with all copies of the Memorandum and Articles of Association issued after the change? ☐

Has the change been advised to staff, customers, suppliers and the authorities? ☐

If change of name is accompanied by change of trade have you ensured no other regulations are being breached? ☐

If name is of particular value has a name watching service been employed to check on similar names being registered? ☐

Does the Board know that the company can dispense with 'limited' in certain circumstances? ☐

If a business name is used, is the appropriate information shown on stationery, etc. and in the business premises? ☐

The Registered Office

■ CHAPTER FIFTEEN ■

Contents

■ KEY QUESTIONS ■

Where may the Registered Office be situated?

Why must the company have a Registered Office?

Must the address of the Registered Office be notified to the Registrar?

When does the change of address of the Registered Office become effective?

Can the change of address registered at Companies House be organised to coincide with the actual move to new premises?

What happens if documents are served at the old address?

Will the company be in breach of the Act if forced out of its Registered Office by circumstances beyond its control?

Does the company name have to be displayed outside the Registered Office?

15:1 Where Registered Office must be situated

Every company must have a Registered Office which must be situated within the jurisdiction of the Companies House with which the company is registered. The regulations with regard to the Registered Office are contained in s.287 of the Companies Act 1985 as amended by s.136 of the Companies Act 1989.

15:2 Need for Registered Office

The address is the one at which legal documents may validly be served and is also the place where the various statutory books should be kept unless the appropriate notice has been given to the Registrar that they are being kept elsewhere.

15:3 Notification of address to Registrar

The address of the first Registered Office must be entered on Form 10 upon incorporation of the company. Any change in the address of the Registered Office must be notified to the Registrar on Form 287, although the Registrar will now accept a change of address from the shuttle Annual Return Form 363s where it is found that the filing of Form 287 has been overlooked. The change becomes effective from the date it is registered by the Registrar.

15:4 Advance notice of change of address

A company may give notice to the Registrar of a proposed change up to 14 days in advance and the change will be effected from the date specified.

15:5 Continuing validity of old address

A document may be validly served at the old Registered Office address for a period of 14 days after the change has been registered. It is, therefore, esssential to have regular inspections of the old Registered Office address to ensure that any documents delivered there after the change has taken place are promptly referred to the appropriate person.

15:6 Enforced move from Registered Office

A company will not be in breach of the Act if it is forced out of its Registered Office without prior warning in circumstances beyond its control and sets up an alternative Registered Office as soon as is practicable and notifies the Registrar within 14 days of so doing.

15:7 Display of company name

The Registered Office is a premises occupied by the company and as such must display the company name outside those premises in accordance with s.348. This applies where the address is solely the Registered Office of the company and is not otherwise occupied by the company for the purpose of running its business, as for example when it is the offices of professional advisors to the company or the private residence of one of the Directors.

■ CHECK LIST ■

Is the Registered Office within the jurisdiction
of Companies House where the company is registered? ☐

The Registered Office is needed as the legal base
of the company. Does the company have a
Registered Office? ☐

Has the address of the Registered Office been notified
to the Registrar? ☐

Has notice been given to Registrar to change on a
fixed date? ☐

The old address is still valid for the service of documents
for 14 days after the move. Have arrangements
been made to check the old address during this period? ☐

The Act will not be breached through a move
forced on the company by circumstances beyond
its control. Does this apply to your company? ☐

Is the company name displayed outside the
Registered Office? ☐

Memorandum and Articles of Association

Contents

■ KEY QUESTIONS ■

Does a company have to have a Memorandum?

What has to be included in the Memorandum?

Can the Memorandum be altered?

What kind of items are covered in the Articles?

Can the company use Table A?

Which Table A applies to the company?

In what form must special Articles be registered?

How does the company alter its Articles?

How often should Articles be updated?

Who should draft new Articles?

What obligations are there on the company when new Articles have been drafted by a third party?

Which Articles govern guarantee companies and unlimited companies?

16:1 Formation of a company

To form a company it is necessary to deliver to the Registrar in Cardiff, for a company whose Registered Office is to be situated in England and Wales, or to the Registrar in Edinburgh, for a company whose Registered Office is to be situated in Scotland, the following documents:

(a) the Memorandum;

(b) the Articles of Association, if it is proposed to register separate Articles;

(c) details of the first Directors of the company;

(d) details of the first Secretary of the company;

(e) consents to act signed by the first Directors and Secretary of the company;

(f) the address of the Registered Office;

(g) a statutory declaration signed by a Solicitor engaged in the formation of the company or by a person named as a Director or the Secretary that all the necessary requirements of registration have been complied with;

(h) a remittance of £20.

Items (c) to (f) are entered on Form 10 and item (g) is completed on Form 12.

If the documents are in order the Registrar will issue a Certificate of Registration and the company is in existence.

16:2 Memorandum

The Memorandum is the constitution of the company and must contain the following information:

(a) name of the company and although this will indicate that the liability of the members is limited by the inclusion of the words 'Limited' or 'Public Limited Company' there must also be a separate statement that the liability of the members is limited;

(b) whether the Registered Office of the company is to be situated in England and Wales or in Scotland. The actual address of the Registered Office is not required;

(c) in the case of a public company the fact that it is a public company;

(d) the Objects of the company: that is the activities in which the company proposes to engage itself;

(e) if the company is a guarantee company there must be a statement that the members undertake to contribute towards the assets of the company up to a certain maximum amount should the company be wound up and be unable to meet its debts. Such an undertaking continues to apply for up to a year after membership ceases for debts incurred whilst that person was a member;

(f) a company with a share capital (except an unlimited company) must state the amount of its share capital and its division into shares of a fixed amount. The minimum issued share capital and therefore the minimum authorised share capital for a public company is £50,000, but this need only be 25 per cent paid-up;

(g) the number of shares taken by each subscriber, that is the persons requesting that the company be incorporated. Each subscriber must take at least one share;

(h) the signature of each subscriber in the presence of one witness, and one witness is sufficient for Scotland as for England and Wales.

16:3 Extent to which Memorandum may be altered

As the company progresses it is probable that some of the items in the Memorandum will require to be altered or updated to meet the changing circumstances of the company. The Memorandum may be altered to the extent set out below:

(a) the name of the company may be altered by special resolution;

(b) the country of residence cannot be altered. A company registered in Cardiff must keep its Registered Office in England and Wales and may not move it to Scotland or move its registration to Scotland. Similarly, a company registered in Scotland must remain registered in Scotland;

(c) the share capital may be increased or reconstructed by ordinary resolution provided the necessary authority to do this has been given in the Articles of Association (*see* **Chapter 18**);

(d)   the Objects of the company may be altered subject to the right of dissident shareholders holding not less than 15 per cent of the voting rights to apply to the Court for any such alteration to be set aside (*see* **Chapter 17**).

16:4   Articles of Association

The Articles are the company's rule book regulating the rights and responsibilities of the members and Directors, and will cover amongst other things:

(a)   the capital structure of the company;

(b)   the issue and transfer of shares;

(c)   the calling and conduct of meetings;

(d)   the appointment and removal of Directors;

(e)   the payment of dividends.

16:5   Application of Table A

A company with a share capital does not have to register Articles and may rely solely upon Table A attached to the Companies Act under which it was registered. A company may register Articles to cover part of its needs and rely for the remainder of its regulations on Table A: alternatively, it may register Articles to specifically exclude the whole or part of Table A. To the extent that Table A has not been excluded or overridden by special Articles it will continue to apply to the company.

The Table A which applies to any company is that attached to the Companies Act under which the company was registered and this will continue to apply even though there may be a subsequent Companies Act with a new Table A, unless the company specifically adopts the Table A of a later Act.

16:6   Registration of special Articles

Where Articles are registered upon incorporation they must be:

(a)   printed;

(b)   divided into paragraphs numbered consecutively;

(c)   signed by each subscriber to the Memorandum in the presence of one witness, and one witness is sufficient for Scotland as for England and Wales.

16:7   Alteration of Articles

A company may alter its Articles by passing a special resolution which is either added to the agenda of the Annual General Meeting or is the subject of an Extraordinary General Meeting called specifically for the purpose.

The notice of the meeting at which it is proposed to change the Articles must state that the resolution is to be proposed as a special resolution and must detail the actual changes which are to be made. If, however, the whole Articles are being re-drawn then it will suffice to refer to a document signed by the Chairman for identification purposes.

If the full changes are not detailed in the resolution then an explanation should be given to the members of the main alterations that are being suggested and the expected effect that they will have on the future running of the company. The full text should be available for those who wish to study it.

16:8   Need to keep Articles up-to-date

A company's Articles should be kept up-to-date and reflect the current practices within the company. This is especially important for a public company with a wide spread of members and it is highly probable that someone will point it out to the company should there be any transgression of the Articles.

It is, however, equally important within a private company that the Articles do reflect the current practices of the company, even though the membership is small and the company operates on a far less formal basis than is generally found within a public company. Should a dispute develop within the membership the majority could possibly find that their wishes are overturned by a minority if the Articles of the company have not been assiduously followed.

16:9   Drafting of revised Articles

If a change in the Articles is proposed it must be decided who is the best person to draft the new Articles. Whilst anyone with a knowledge of the Companies Act and a command of the English language should be able to undertake the task it is often felt desirable to delegate the work to Solicitors or Accountants who have a Company Secretarial department. This will usually mean that it will be undertaken by persons with experience of this work who should be able to draw on their experience of other companies' requirements in this direction.

One duty that the Company Secretary cannot delegate, however, is the specification of the changes that are required and the checking of the finished product to see that it does properly detail the regulations requested. The Articles are a working document and it is essential that they are written in readable English and that the meaning is not obscured by legal jargon which is unnecessary and should not be tolerated.

16:10   Articles of guarantee companies and unlimited companies

Guarantee companies and unlimited companies must register Articles upon incorporation because they are not governed by Table A. They must either register special Articles or adopt the appropriate specimen Articles attached to the Companies Act under which they are incorporated as detailed below:

- **Company limited by guarantee without a share capital should use Table C.**

- **Company limited by guarantee with a share capital should use Table D.**

- **Unlimited company with a share capital should use Table E.**

■ CHECK LIST ■

The Memorandum is an essential document for the formation of a company. ☐

The Memorandum is the constitution of the company and sets out the Objects for which it has been formed. ☐

The Memorandum can be changed within certain limits to reflect the changing circumstances of the company. ☐

The Articles of Association are the rule book of the company and govern relations between the members and Directors. ☐

Table A applies to all limited companies with a share capital unless specifically excluded. ☐

The Articles may be altered by special resolution. ☐

The Articles should be kept up-to-date and reflect current practices within the company. ☐

When changing the Articles it is the company's responsibility to detail specific regulations required to meet their particular circumstances. ☐

It is the company's responsibility to ensure revised Articles do give the rules required and are written in readable English. ☐

Guarantee companies and unlimited companies should adopt Table C, D or E as appropriate. ☐

The Objects Clause and *Ultra Vires*

■ CHAPTER SEVENTEEN ■

Contents

■ KEY QUESTIONS ■

What is meant by *Ultra Vires*?

Why is the Objects Clause usually so extensive and is it necessary?

Can the company adopt the new simplified Objects Clause?

Are there any disadvantages from using the new Objects Clause?

Are there any advantages from using the new Objects Clause?

To what extent can the Objects Clause be altered?

Does a dissentient minority have any rights on a change of Objects?

What happens to a resolution to change the Objects if an application is made to the Court?

How does a company proceed to change its Objects?

What items should be considered if there is to be a complete change of trade?

What is the current position on a contract which is found to be *Ultra Vires*?

Are there any exceptions to these rules?

What can the company do if it is found to have committed an *Ultra Vires* act?

17:1 Importance of Objects Clause

The Memorandum of the company must contain amongst other matters the Objects for which the company has been formed. The company may only engage in those activities which are covered by its Objects Clause and to enter into any contractual obligations outside those objects is acting *Ultra Vires* or beyond the powers of the Directors and the company.

17:2 Current practice with regard to Objects Clause

In the early days of company formations the Objects Clause was a fairly simple statement but over the years it has become a much longer and more detailed list of activities permitted to the company. This has come from the wish to ensure that the company did not breach the *Ultra Vires* rules, the limited ability to change a company's Objects until the introduction of the relevant sections of the 1989 Companies Act, and to encompass the general increase in commercial activity that has taken place where companies now have far wider horizons than in years past.

It has been common practice to list in the Objects Clause all the activities in which the company may possibly wish to engage itself, often very remote from the industries in which the main trading is conducted, and the powers that the company will require to achieve those Objects, such as the power to employ staff, pay pensions, open Bank accounts, for example. The Objects Clause is therefore often a very long statement taking up several sheets of paper.

17:3 Simplified Objects Clause

Section 3A introduced into the 1985 Act by s.110 of the 1989 Act says that where the company's Memorandum states that the company is to carry on business as a general commercial company then it may carry on any trade or business whatsoever and has the power to do all such things as are incidental or conducive to carrying on any trade or business by the company. It is therefore now possible for the Objects Clause to be a very brief statement.

Whilst the adoption of this new simplified form of Objects Clause would seem to remove any possibility of a company ever trading *Ultra Vires* it appears not to have found universal approval with some bankers and with some sections of the legal profession who prefer that a company's powers be specifically set down. Where a company has power to do all things 'incidental' or 'conducive' to carrying on a trade there could possibly be legal argument as to the extent of the meaning of these two words in any particular case.

It would seem, however, that the addition of this new clause to an existing full length Objects Clause could prevent a company inadvertently acting *Ultra Vires*. The use of this new abbreviated Objects Clause in this manner as a safety net should be considered.

17:4 Change of Objects Clause

Section 4 of the 1985 Act as amended by s.110(2) of the 1989 Act allows the Objects Clause to be altered by special resolution to any extent whatsoever. Prior to the introduction of these amendments the ability of a company to alter its Objects Clause was limited, but those restrictions have been removed and a company may now alter its Objects Clause however it wishes, even to a complete change of trade.

Section 5 stipulates, however, that holders of 15 per cent of the share capital who did not vote for the resolution to change the Objects Clause may apply to the Court to have the resolution set aside. Any such application must be made to the Court within 21 days of the resolution being passed. The Court may disallow the proposed change or allow it in full or in part on any terms or conditions which it sees fit to impose.

17:5 Filing resolution to change Objects Clause

Within 15 days of passing the resolution, a copy must be filed with Companies House

If no application is made to the Court within 21 days of it being passed to have the resolution set aside, then within a further 15 days the company must deliver to the Registrar a printed copy of the Memorandum as altered.

If application is made to the Court to have the resolution set aside then the company must forthwith file with the Registrar Form 6 notifying him that an application has been made. Within 15 days of the Court delivering its decision the company must file with the Registrar an office copy of the Court order and if the resolution is approved also file a printed copy of the Memorandum as altered. If the Court refuses to allow the changes to be implemented the company has only to file the copy of the Court order because no changes to the Memorandum have actually taken place.

17:6   Procedure for altering Objects Clause

As previously stated, a resolution to alter the Objects Clause of the Memorandum must be a special resolution added to the Agenda of the Annual General Meeting or proposed at an Extraordinary General Meeting called specially for the purpose.

The notice of the meeting must state that the resolution is to be moved as a special resolution and the wording of the resolution must be set out in the notice of the meeting. The resolution must specify the actual alterations that are being made unless the whole Objects Clause is being re-written, when it will be sufficient to refer to a document signed by the Chairman for identification purposes.

If the changes are not self-evident from the wording of the resolution then it would be good practice to accompany the notice of the meeting with a letter from the Chairman explaining the nature and consequences of the changes. The shareholders should also be given the opportunity of obtaining a copy of the full document where this has not been circulated to all members.

17:7   Complete change of trade

If the changes amount to a complete change of trade for the company, care should be given to other consequences of such actions. Principal items for consideration would include:

(a)   are there any loans from the Bank or other source which are tied to the pursuit of any particular trade or business?

(b) will the use of existing premises for following a new trade require permission from the planning authorities?

(c) are there any tax losses available to be brought forward to be set off against future profits which would be lost if there was a change of trade?

17:8 *Ultra Vires*

As previously stated, a company may only engage in any activity specifically allowed under its Objects Clause of the Memorandum and any action by the company outside the scope of this clause is *Ultra Vires*.

Until the introduction of the European Communities Act 1972 any contract which was *Ultra Vires* was void. The company did not have the power for its Directors to complete the company's part of the agreement and the contract was totally unenforceable in the Courts. The thinking behind this concept was that anyone contracting with a company had the opportunity to satisfy themselves that the proposed contract was in accordance with the permitted activities of the company by inspecting the Memorandum held on the Registrar's file at Companies House.

17:8.1 *Current limitations of* Ultra Vires

The impracticalities of this position have been recognised and s.35 of the 1985 Act as amended by s.108 of the 1989 Act restricts the operation of the *Ultra Vires* principle so that a third party contracting with the company in good faith may assume that the Directors are acting within their powers and any consequent contract is therefore valid. Whilst *Ultra Vires* is now virtually non-existent as far as normal commercial transactions are concerned the principle still exists in the following situations:

(a) where a Director contracts with the company in his/her private capacity and it is found that the contract is *Ultra Vires* then it will be voidable at the instance of the company. That is, the Director will be bound to the contract though the company may default from it if they so wish;

(b) where an action planned by the Directors is thought to be *Ultra Vires* a shareholder may petition the Court to prevent the Directors carrying out such an act;

(c)   where a company has carried out an *Ultra Vires* act a shareholder who considers he/she has lost through this action may petition the Court to seek damages against the Directors to redress these losses.

17:9   Ratification of an *Ultra Vires* act

Where an *Ultra Vires* act has been carried out it may be ratified by the members in general meeting by special resolution. Similarly, the Directors may be absolved from any liability for having carried out an *Ultra Vires* act by special resolution passed by the members in a general meeting and this must be a separate resolution from that ratifying their actions.

■ CHECK LIST ■

Are the company's activities limited to those items listed in the Objects Clause? ☐

Is the Objects Clause drawn very widely? ☐

Has the company adopted a simplified Objects Clause? ☐

Is it possible that the simplified Objects Clause could give rise to doubt as to the actual powers of the company? ☐

Has the new clause been added to existing Objects to ensure that Directors never act Ultra Vires? ☐

Is everyone aware that the Objects Clause may now be changed without restriction? ☐

Is it likely that a dissident minority will apply to the Court to have a change of Objects set aside? ☐

Has a special resolution been passed to effect a change of the Objects Clause? ☐

Special regulations apply to filing a copy resolution if application is made to the Court to have it set aside. Do you know what they are? ☐

Are you aware that *Ultra Vires*:

(a) is no longer effective in normal trading? ☐

(b) still exists between Directors and members? ☐

(c) actions can be ratified by special resolution? ☐

Increase or reconstruction of capital

■ CHAPTER EIGHTEEN ■

Contents

■ KEY QUESTIONS ■

What is the authorised capital and is there any minimum amount stipulated?

Does the minimum issued capital of a public company have to be subscribed at the time of issue of the Certificate to Commence Trading?

Can the authorised capital be altered?

What is meant by reconstruction of capital?

What resolutions and forms have to be filed with Companies House on the alteration of the authorised capital?

18:1 Authorised capital

Every company must state in its Memorandum the amount of its authorised capital and its division into shares of a fixed amount. In the case of a public company it may not proceed to commence trading until it receives from the Registrar the appropriate certificate which will be issued when the Registrar has been satisfied through the receipt of Form 117 that share capital to the nominal amount of £50,000 has been issued, though the initial payment need only be 25 per cent of the nominal value plus any premium. A public company must, therefore, have a minimum authorised capital of £50,000, but apart from this there are no restrictions on the amount of authorised capital any company may have.

Companies House has pointed out that the minimum issued capital must be subscribed and that an undertaking to subscribe will not satisfy the legislation.

18:2 Alteration of authorised capital

By s.121 of the Companies Act 1985 a company may alter the amount of its share capital or its division into shares of a fixed amount as stated in its Memorandum provided the necessary authority to effect an alteration is given in the Articles of Association. The alteration is carried out by the members passing an ordinary resolution in general meeting.

The resolution may be added to the agenda of the Annual General Meeting or be the subject of an Extraordinary General Meeting called specifically for the purpose. The notice of the meeting should print the actual wording of the resolution to be proposed which should detail the changes to be made.

The changes can be for any of the following purposes:

(a)   to increase the share capital by the creation of new shares. This action increases the authorised share capital only and gives the Directors the ability to issue further shares, but the actual issue of those shares is a separate operation;

(b)   to consolidate its shares and divide them into new shares of a larger amount than they were originally;

(c)   to convert its paid-up shares into stock;

(d)   to reconvert stock into shares of any denomination;

(e)   to sub-divide the shares into shares of a smaller nominal value. If the shares are partly paid, the proportion unpaid on the new shares must be the same proportion of the nominal amount as with the original shares;

(f)   to cancel any shares which at that time have not been taken or agreed to be taken and reduce the authorised capital accordingly. Such a cancellation is not regarded as a reduction of share capital which refers to issued share capital.

18:3   Filing notification of alteration

Where a resolution to increase the authorised share capital has been passed there must be filed with the Registrar within 15 days of the resolution being passed a copy of the resolution together with a copy of Form 123.

Where a resolution has been passed to alter the share capital in any of the ways listed above, apart from increasing it, there must be filed with the Registrar within one month of the resolution being passed a copy of Form 122 detailing the changes that have been made.

■ CHECK LIST ■

Is authorised capital as shown in the Memorandum? ☐

Is the issued and therefore also authorised
capital for a public company at least £50,000? ☐

Has the minimum issued capital for a public company
been subscribed? An undertaking to subscribe
will not suffice. ☐

Is authority given in the Articles to alter the authorised
capital by ordinary resolution? ☐

Can the alteration be to increase or reconstruct
the capital? ☐

Where the capital is increased, has a copy resolution
been filed together with the appropriate form? ☐

Where the capital is reconstructed, has the
appropriate form been filed? ☐

Issued share capital

■ **CHAPTER NINETEEN** ■

Contents

■ KEY QUESTIONS ■

What is the effect of having an authorised capital?

What limits are there on the Directors' authority to issue shares?

How is that authority given to the Directors?

Does the grant of a right to subscribe for shares count as an issue of shares?

Must there be consideration for an issue of shares and does it have to be cash?

Does a return have to be made to Companies House of shares allotted?

What are pre-emption rights?

Can pre-emption rights be set aside?

To whom can a private company make a general offer of shares?

Can shares be offered for sale at a discount?

Can shares be offered for sale at a premium?

Can shares be issued partly paid?

Can the company pay underwriting commission?

What forms can non cash consideration take?

Is a bonus issue made for a non cash consideration?

Can goodwill form part of a non cash consideration?

What must a public company do if it loses more than half of its capital?

In what ways can a company reduce its capital?

Can creditors object to a reduction of capital?

Can a company issue redeemable equity shares?

What restrictions are there on the redemption of equity shares?

Can a company purchase its own shares?

■ KEY QUESTIONS ■

May the shares purchased by the company be re-issued?

What amounts have to be transferred to the Capital Redemption Reserve?

Can redemption be out of capital?

Can members and creditors object to redemption out of capital?

Can a company give financial assistance for the purchase of its own shares?

19:1   Introduction

The Memorandum of the company states the amount of the authorised share capital of the company though this does not all have to be issued and in many companies a surplus of unissued capital is left available for future use as the needs of the company dictate. If, when an issue of shares is contemplated, it is found that the authorised share capital is inadequate to encompass the proposed new shares then the authorised capital will have to be increased before the issue of shares can proceed.

19:2   Directors' authority to allot shares

Within the limits set by the authorised capital the Directors may allot shares when authorised by the company in general meeting or when authorised by the Articles of Association and any allotment must be in accordance with s.80. Any authority given to the Directors to allot shares, whether it be given in the Articles or by the company in general meeting, must state the maximum number of securities that may be issued and the date that the authority expires which must not exceed five years from the date when it was given, except that a private company may now pass an elective resolution for that authority to be of an indefinite period (s.80A (s.115, CA 1989)).

Any authority given to the Directors initially or any renewal may be given by ordinary resolution even if this amounts to an alteration of the Articles, and under s.380 a copy of any such resolution even though it is an ordinary resolution must be filed with the Registrar within 15 days of being passed.

These regulations regarding the authority of Directors to allot shares do not apply to shares issued in accordance with the Memorandum which must be issued to the subscribers to the Memorandum or to shares issued in accordance with the terms of an Employees' Share Scheme.

19:3   Grant of rights to subscribe

The grant of a right, or an option, to subscribe for shares is equivalent to an issue of shares and must be covered by the authority to allot shares given to the Directors at the time that the option is granted. Should the subsequent issue of shares take place after the expiry of the Directors' authority to allot shares but be made in accordance with an agreement concluded within their period of authority then that issue will be perfectly valid.

19:4 Consideration for issue of shares

Any issue of shares by the Directors must be for a consideration. That consideration may be cash or in some form other than cash. Shares issued for cash will take the form of a rights issue or an offer for sale, whereas shares issued for a consideration other than cash will usually be in the form of a bonus issue to existing shareholders or the purchase of another business or of specific assets.

19:5 Return of allotments

Within one month of the issue of shares a return of allotments must be made to the Registrar on Form 88(2). If the total number of shares to be issued have not all been allotted within a space of one month it will be necessary to file Form 88(2) listing those shares allotted and to continue to file Form 88(2) each month until the issue has been completed.

Where the consideration for the issue of the shares was not cash then a copy of the contract stamped, if appropriate, in accordance with Inland Revenue regulations must accompany Form 88(2). If the contract was not in writing then details of the terms upon which the shares were allotted must be entered on Form 88(3), which itself must be stamped, if appropriate, by the Inland Revenue, and filed with Form 88(2).

19:6 Pre-emption rights

Under s.89 shares offered for payment in cash should be offered on a pre-emptive basis, that is to existing shareholders in proportion to their existing holdings. These provisions may be set aside by a power in the Articles, or in the Memorandum in the case of a private company, or by a special resolution for any company.

Where a resolution to disapply pre-emption rights is proposed for a specific issue as opposed to being applied generally, then it must be accompanied by a statement from the Directors giving their reasons for their recommendation, the amount to be received from the issue and the Directors' justification of that amount (s.95).

The Directors' powers to set aside pre-emption rights will expire when their authority to issue shares expires. Both powers may be renewed by passing in general meeting the appropriate resolutions.

19:7   Offer of shares to the public

In the case of a public company making a general offer for sale there are restrictions imposed by the Stock Exchange and the Financial Services Act 1986 so that the shares may only be allotted if the minimum subscription stipulated in the offer documents is received and that permission is received from the Stock Exchange for dealings in those shares to take place.

It is an offence for a private company to offer its shares or debentures to the public. In this connection 'the public' does not include existing members, employees, members of the families of existing members or employees or debenture holders. Persons outside this group of connected people could be approached to become members of a private company but only on an individual basis and not through a general offer for sale.

19:8   Shares may not be offered at a discount

Shares offered for sale for cash may be offered at par value or at some higher figure. Shares may not be issued at a discount though this restriction does not apply to the issue of debentures.

19:9 Shares may be offered at a premium

If the shares are issued at a price above par then any surplus over the nominal value of the shares must be placed to a share premium account to which restrictions are applied as to the use to which it may be put.

19:10 Partly paid shares

Shares need not be paid in full upon issue but may be partly paid with further calls to be made at fixed dates or at the Directors' discretion. By s.101 a public company may not allot shares until a minimum subscription of 25 per cent of the nominal value of the shares plus any premium has been paid.

19:11 Underwriting commission

By s.97 a company may pay commission to persons subscribing or procuring others to subscribe for shares provided authority is given in the Articles and the rate does not exceed ten per cent of the issue price or such lesser sum stated in the Articles.

19:12 Bonus issue

One form of issue of shares for a non cash consideration would be a bonus issue of shares. A bonus issue takes place when the company uses sums standing to the credit of reserves in the company's balance sheet or uses profits otherwise available for distribution to the members of the company to pay for shares which are then distributed to the holders of the equity in proportion to their existing holdings.

The consideration, being the nominal value of the shares issued in this way, will be transferred from the reserves in which it is currently standing to the capital account. This money will then no longer be available for distribution and must be treated in the manner stipulated to ensure the maintenance of the company's capital.

19:13 Goodwill

Shares may otherwise be issued for a non cash consideration when a business or specific assets are purchased. The purchase price may include goodwill and 'know–how' and will almost certainly include some elements of this in the purchase of a going concern business.

In the case of a public company, certain other restrictions are imposed regarding the consideration for the issue of shares:

(a) assets acquired must be the subject of an independent valuation (s.108);

(b) where the consideration consists in whole or in part of an undertaking that undertaking must be completed within five years (s.102);

(c) the consideration must not include a promise to do work or perform services (s.99).

19:14 Loss of capital

Where a public company finds it has lost capital to the extent that the net assets represent a half or less of the called-up share capital the Directors must within 28 days of becoming aware of the fact call an Extraordinary General Meeting to be held within a further 56 days to consider what measures, if any, should be taken. The Act does not specify any resolutions to be put before the meeting and merely holding the meeting will ensure compliance.

19:15 Reduction of share capital

A company may reduce its share capital by special resolution where authority is given in the Articles and subject to the confirmation of the Court (s.135). The reduction may be made in the following ways:

(a) extinguish or reduce any liability in connection with unpaid capital;

(b) cancel any paid-up share capital which is lost or is not represented by assets;

(c)   pay off any paid-up share capital which is surplus to the company's requirements.

Any creditor of the company is entitled to object to the reduction when it comes before the Court for confirmation if the reduction involves diminishing unpaid share capital or the repayment of surplus share capital. A copy of a Court order confirming a reduction of capital must be filed with the Registrar.

19:16   Redeemable equity shares

Alternative methods of reducing share capital are now available under s.159 and s.162.

By s.159 a company may issue redeemable equity shares provided authority is given in the Articles. At the time of issue there must be in existence some non-redeemable equity shares and the shares may only be redeemed if they are fully paid. The date or dates upon which the shares may be redeemed must be stated in the Articles or, if delegated to the Directors, must be fixed prior to the issue of the shares. Any other circumstances in which the shares may be redeemed must be stated in the Articles.

The amount payable upon redemption or the basis upon which it is calculated must be stated in the Articles and it must not be subject to a person's discretion or opinion. Redemption must be made out of distributable profits or the proceeds of a fresh issue of shares and any premium on redemption must be made out of distributable profits unless the shares were issued at a premium when the proceeds of a fresh issue of shares may be used.

Any shares redeemed must be cancelled and this is a reduction of issued capital: it does not reduce the authorised capital. A private company may make redemption out of capital – *see* 19:20 below.

19:17   Purchase of own shares

Under s.162 a company may purchase its own shares subject to the power to do so being contained in the Articles. The purchases when completed must always leave in existence some non-redeemable equity shares. The purchases may be made in the stock market by public companies with a stock exchange quotation, or otherwise by private treaty.

The authority to purchase must be given by special resolution in advance of entry into any agreement to purchase. Any shares so purchased must be cancelled.

Where the authority is for market purchases the resolution must also specify the maximum number of shares which may be acquired and the maximum and minimum price which may be paid. An expiry date for the authority must also be quoted which may not be more than 18 months after the date on which the resolution is passed.

Where the authority is to acquire shares by private treaty the proposed contracts to purchase the shares must be available for inspection at the Registered Office of the company for 15 days prior to the meeting and at the meeting itself.

19:18   Returns to Companies House

A return of any shares purchased must be made to the Registrar within 28 days of purchase on Form 169, which is subject to Inland Revenue stamp duty. There are also corporation tax implications if the shares are purchased at a premium to their nominal value. The company must retain at its Registered Office for a period of ten years a copy of any contract to purchase shares and where the contract is not in writing a memorandum of its terms. The copy contracts and memoranda are open to inspection by members of the company and in the case of public companies by members of the public.

19:19   Transfer to Capital Redemption Reserve

Where the shares are redeemed or purchased out of profits then an equivalent amount must be transferred to a Capital Redemption Reserve. Where the redemption or purchase is made partly out of profits and partly out of the proceeds of a fresh issue of shares then any excess of the purchase price over the proceeds of the new issue must be placed to a Capital Redemption Reserve.

19:20   Redemption out of capital

A private company, if authorised by its Articles, may redeem or purchase its own shares out of capital. Section 173 states that the purchase must be approved by a special resolution and the Directors must make a statutory declaration on Form 173 that after the payment the company will be able to meet its debts and that in their opinion the company will be able to continue as a going concern for the following year. This statutory declaration must be supported by a statement by the Auditors.

The statutory declaration and the Auditors' report must be available for inspection at the meeting at which the special resolution is proposed. The statutory declaration must be made within the week immediately preceeding the date that the resolution is passed and the purchase or the redemption of the shares must take place not less than five weeks nor more than seven weeks after the resolution is passed.

Where a member whose shares are to be redeemed or purchased votes in favour of the resolution the resolution will be ineffective if it would have failed without that member's support.

A return of shares redeemed or purchased out of capital must be made to the Registrar on Form 169 within 28 days of the purchase.

19:21   Public notice for redemption out of capital

Within one week of the passing of the resolution to redeem or purchase its own shares out of capital the company must publish a notice in the *Gazette* stating that:

(a)   the resolution has been approved;

(b)   the amount of the approved capital payment;

(c)   the statutory declaration and the Auditors' report are available for inspection at the Registered Office;

(d)   any creditor may within five weeks of the date that the resolution was passed make application to the Court for the resolution to be set aside.

Also within a week of the resolution being passed, the company must place a similar advertisement in a national newspaper or write to all the creditors, and send a copy of the statutory declaration and the Auditors' report to the Registrar. For a further five weeks the statutory declaration and the Auditors' report must be kept at the Registered Office and made available for inspection by members and creditors free of charge.

19:22 Members and creditors may apply to the Court

Within five weeks of the passing of the resolution any member who did not vote in favour of the resolution or any creditor may make application to the Court for the resolution to be set aside. The company must forthwith notify the Registrar that an application has been made to the Court and within 15 days of the Court delivering its decision send a copy of the Court order to Companies House. The Court may approve the resolution or make an order on such terms as it thinks fit.

19:23 Financial assistance to acquire shares

In general terms, s.151 prohibits the giving of assistance to a member to purchase shares in the company. The giving of assistance has a wide meaning and extends beyond merely lending money and covers any transaction which is not a normal commercial one.

The rules are relaxed in the case of a private company by s.155 which states that such assistance must be approved by a special resolution and that the payment must be made out of distributable profits. The Directors must provide a statutory declaration on Form 155(6)(A) or 155(6)(B) stating that the company is able to meet its debts which must be supported by an Auditors' report. Copies of all these documents must be filed with the Registrar within 15 days of the resolution being passed.

■ CHECK LIST ■

Is the authorised capital sufficient to cover
any proposed issue of shares? ☐

Do the Directors have authority to issue any shares? ☐

Does the Directors' authority exceed five years? ☐

Has the ordinary resolution giving Directors the authority
to issue shares been filed at Companies House? ☐

Is the grant of a right to subscribe for shares covered
by the Directors' authority to issue shares at the
time the right is granted? ☐

Does consideration exist for an issue of shares? ☐

Has a return of allotments been made to Companies
House? ☐

Are you aware that pre-emption rights apply to an
offer for sale of shares for cash? ☐

Are you aware that it is an offence for a private
company to offer its shares to the public? ☐

Do you know that shares may not be issued at a discount? ☐

Are you aware that shares may be issued at a premium? ☐

Do you know that shares may be issued partly paid? ☐

Are you aware that underwriting commission may be paid? ☐

Are you aware that shares may be issued as a bonus
issue to existing members? ☐

Did you know that goodwill can form part of the
consideration when shares are issued for other
than cash? ☐

When a public company has lost more than half
of its capital a general meeting must be called
to discuss the situation. Has this been done? ☐

Has the Court confirmed that share capital may be reduced? ☐

■ CHECK LIST ■

Redeemable equity shares may be issued. Do you
  wish to do this? ☐

Have you cancelled any of the company's own shares
  which have recently been purchased? ☐

Has a return been made to Companies House of all
  shares which have been purchased and cancelled? ☐

Has an equivalent amount to the cost of the purchases
  been transferred to a Capital Redemption Reserve? ☐

Has the purchase of own shares been made out of capital
  by a private company? ☐

Members and creditors can apply to the Court where
  redemption is out of capital. Were you aware of this? ☐

Normally, a company may not give assistance for a
  person to acquire shares in the company.
  Does your company do this? ☐

Were you aware that the rules on financial assistance
  may be relaxed for a private company? ☐

Registration of charges

■ **CHAPTER TWENTY** ■

Contents

■ KEY QUESTIONS ■

What are the consequences of not registering a charge at Companies House?

What is the time limit for registering a charge at Companies House?

What information on registered charges has to be kept by the company?

How is the satisfaction of a charge notified to Companies House?

If a Receiver is appointed under a charge does Companies House have to be advised?

20:1 Need to register charges with Companies House

The law as it currently stands provides that any charge on a company's property or assets is void against a liquidator or creditor if it is not registered at Companies House within 21 days of its creation. It is the company's responsibility to register any charge but it is common practice for the chargee to undertake this in order to ensure that the registration is carried out within the time limits and that the charge is valid against a liquidator and other creditors. A filing fee of £10 is now payable for the registration of a charge. If a charge is void due to late registration then the money secured by it becomes immediately re-payable.

A copy of the instrument creating the charge or, in the case of a series of debentures, one of the series must be deposited with Companies House which will keep the details on the company's file and also issue a certificate of registration of the charge (s.395 *et seq.* for companies registered in England and Wales and s.410 *et seq.* for companies registered in Scotland). The Certificate of Registration will be sent to the person registering the charge and if not the company, a copy of the certificate should be obtained for retention at the Registered Office.

20:2 Register of Charges

The company must keep at its Registered Office a Register of Charges and a copy of every instrument evidencing a charge or, in the case of a series of debentures, one of the series. The Register must show brief details of the property charged, the beneficiaries and the amount of the charge. The Register and copy instruments are open to inspection (*see* **Chapter 1**).

20:3 Notification of satisfaction of charge

When a charge is satisfied, notification is made to the Registrar on Form 403(a) for companies registered in England and Wales and on Form 419(a) for companies registered in Scotland. An Officer of the company has to make a statutory declaration when submitting these forms and in respect of Form 419(a) the verification of the chargee is required in respect of a floating charge.

20:4   Notification of appointment of Receiver

Where a Receiver or Manager is appointed to a company in accordance with the terms of a charge, notification must be given to the Registrar within seven days of his/her appointment. Similarly, when a Receiver or Manager ceases to act notification must be given to the Registrar.

20:5   New provisions to be introduced

Completely new provisions with regard to the registration of charges are, however, set out in the Companies Act 1989 in s.92 *et seq*. It is thought unlikely though that they will be introduced in the form set out in the Act and a consultation document has been issued.

■ CHECK LIST ■

A charge must be registered within 21 days of
creation otherwise it is void. Has this been done? ☐

Have copies of instruments creating a charge been
deposited at Companies House? ☐

Does the company keep a Register of all charges
and copies of the instruments creating the charges? ☐

Does the company have copies of all Certificates
of Registration? ☐

Has the satisfaction of a charge been notified to
Companies House by filing the appropriate form? ☐

Has the notification of the appointment of a Receiver under
a charge been made to Companies House
within seven days of the appointment? ☐

Re-registration

■ **CHAPTER TWENTY-ONE** ■

Contents

■ KEY QUESTIONS ■

PRIVATE COMPANY RE-REGISTERED AS A PUBLIC
COMPANY

May any private company re-register as a public company?

Do the Memorandum and Articles have to be altered?

Do the Memorandum and Articles have to be reprinted?

Are there any relevant financial considerations to be satisfied prior
to the change?

Do the Auditors have to report on the company?

Are there any other specialist reports which are required?

What capital requirements have to be complied with prior to the
change?

When does the change become effective?

PUBLIC COMPANY RE-REGISTERED AS A PRIVATE
COMPANY

May a public company re-register as a company limited by shares
or by guarantee?

Do the Memorandum and Articles have to be altered?

What rights are available to members who are not in favour of the
change?

If dissident members apply to the Court does the company have
to notify the Registrar?

If no successful challenge to the change in the Memorandum and
Articles is mounted do they have to be reprinted?

When does the change become effective?

LIMITED COMPANY RE-REGISTERED AS AN
UNLIMITED COMPANY

May any limited company re-register as unlimited?

Do the Memorandum and Articles have to be altered?

■ KEY QUESTIONS ■

What proportion of members have to agree to the change?

Do the Memorandum and Articles have to be reprinted?

When does the change become effective?

UNLIMITED COMPANY RE-REGISTERED AS A LIMITED COMPANY

May any unlimited company re-register as limited?

May an unlimited company become a public company?

Do the Memorandum and Articles have to be altered?

Do the Memorandum and Articles have to be reprinted?

What are the time limits for filing the resolution to change the Memorandum and Articles and the application to change the status of the company?

21:1 Re-registration of private company as public

The requirements whereby a private company may re-register as a public company are set out in s.43 and the sections following it. A company can not be re-registered as public if it has previously been re-registered as unlimited.

21:1.1 Need to pass a special resolution

To re-register the company must pass a special resolution to:

(a) alter the Memorandum so that it states that the company is a public company;

(b) alter the Memorandum as necessary to comply with the regulations for a public company. This would include compliance with share capital requirements for a public company and change of name to end with 'Public limited company' and may also change the name to remove the word 'company' or the words 'and company';

(c) alter the Articles as necessary. This would include, if appropriate, the removal of restrictions on the number of members and the Directors' right to refuse to register a transfer of shares.

21:1.2 Documents to be filed

The company must then file with the Registrar the following documents:

(a) Form 43(3) signed by a Director or by the Company Secretary;

(b) a printed copy of the Memorandum and Articles as amended by special resolution as mentioned above;

(c) a copy of a written statement from the Auditors that the relevant balance sheet shows that the net assets exceed the sum of the called-up share capital and the undistributable reserves as defined in s.264(2);

(d) a copy of the relevant balance sheet together with an unqualified Auditors' Report made up to a date not more than seven months prior to the date of the application;

(e) a copy of the valuation report required under s.44 (see below) if applicable;

(f)   a statutory declaration on Form 43(3)(e) made by a Director or by the Company Secretary.

21:1.3   Valuation of consideration for shares

Where the company has allotted shares between the date of the relevant balance sheet and the date that the resolution was passed under s.43 and those shares were fully or partly paid up otherwise than in cash, except where reserves or the balance standing to the profit and loss account have been capitalised, then by s.44:

(a)   the consideration for the allotment must be valued by an independent expert in accordance with s.108;

(b)   the report of the valuation must have been made to the company within the six months preceeding the allotment.

21:1.4   Capital requirements for re-registration

At the time that the company passes the special resolution under s.43 it must ensure that:

(a)   it has a minimum issued share capital of £50,000;

(b)   any partly paid shares, other than shares issued under an Employees Share Scheme, are paid up to the extent of 25 per cent of their nominal value plus any premium;

(c)   where the consideration for an allotment of shares included a promise to do work or perform services, that the work or service has been completed or the consideration otherwise discharged;

(d)   where the consideration for an allotment of shares included an undertaking, that undertaking must have been discharged or there must be a contract in existence for it to be discharged within five years.

21:1.5   Registrar's Certificate

When the Registrar is satisfied that the application complies with the requirements of s.43 he will issue a Certificate of Incorporation stating that the company is a public company. It is at this point that the change becomes effective and the special resolutions amending the Memorandum and Articles take effect.

21:2 Re-registration of public company as private

The requirements whereby a public company may re-register as a private company are set out in s.53 and the following sections. A public company may re-register as a private company limited by shares or by guarantee.

21:2.1 Need for special resolution

A company wishing to re-register must pass a special resolution to alter the Memorandum so that it no longer states that the company is a public company and to make any other amendments to the Memorandum or Articles as may be necessary.

21:2.2 Right of dissident members to apply to the Court

There are rights for members who are not in favour of the change to make application to the Court for the resolution to be set aside.

Section 54 states that where a public company has passed a special resolution to re-register as a private company an application to the Court for the cancellation of that resolution may be made:

(a)   by one or more of their number appointed in writing on behalf of:

    (i)   holders of not less than five per cent of the issued share capital or any class thereof; or

    (ii)   not less than 50 members;

(b)   within 28 days of the date that the resolution was passed,

but *not* by anyone who voted in favour of, or consented to, the resolution.

If an application is made to the Court the company must forthwith notify the Registrar on Form 54. The Court will confirm or cancel the resolution or allow it to proceed on such terms and conditions as it thinks fit. The company must file with the Registrar a copy of the Court Order within 15 days of it being made or within such longer time as may be allowed by the Court.

21:2.3 Special resolution cleared prior to re-registration

When application is made to the Registrar to re-register the company then:

(a) the special resolution must not have been cancelled by order of the Court;

(b) the period during which application may be made to the Court has expired without an application having been made; or

(c) an application has been made to the Court and has either been withdrawn or the Court has made an order under s.54 confirming the resolution and a copy of that order has been filed with the Registrar.

21:2.4 Documents to be filed

When the resolution has been passed and the conditions above have been met the actual application to re-register is made on Form 53 signed by a Director or the Company Secretary and filed with the Registrar together with a printed copy of the Memorandum and Articles as altered by the resolution.

21:2.5 Registrar's Certificate

The Registrar will issue a Certificate of Incorporation as a private company and it is at that point that the change becomes effective and the amendments to the Memorandum and Articles take effect.

21:3 Re-registration of limited company as unlimited

The regulations whereby a limited company may re-register as unlimited are set out in ss.49 and 50. These provisions do not allow re-registration by a company which was unlimited and has re-registered as limited, or by a public company or any company which has previously been re-registered as unlimited.

The application must be made on Form 49(1) and must show the alterations to the Memorandum and the alterations to the Articles necessary for the company to comply with the Act as an unlimited company. If Articles have not been previously registered then Articles must be annexed to Form 49(1).

The following documents must be filed with the Registrar:

(a) Form 49(1) signed by a Director or by the Secretary;

(b) Form 49(8)(A) signed by or on behalf of *all* members of the company assenting to the re-registration as an unlimited company;

(c) Form 49(8)(B) being a statutory declaration made by the Directors;

(d) a printed copy of the Memorandum as amended;

(e) a printed copy of the Articles as amended, if Articles had been previously registered.

The Registrar will issue a Certificate of Incorporation as an unlimited company and it is at that point that the change becomes effective and the revised Memorandum and Articles take effect.

21:4   Re-registration of unlimited company as limited

The regulations whereby an unlimited company may re-register as a limited company are set out in ss.51 and 52. A company may not be re-registered as a public company nor may a company re-register as limited if it has previously been re-registered as unlimited.

The company must pass a special resolution to amend the Memorandum and the Articles as is necessary in the circumstances if it is to be limited by shares, or to amend the Memorandum and Articles if it is to be limited by guarantee. A copy of the resolution must be filed with the Registrar within 15 days of being passed under s.380.

The following documents must be filed with the Registrar not earlier than the copy resolution mentioned above is received by him:

(a) Form 51, being an application to re-register signed by a Director or by the Secretary;

(b) a printed copy of the Memorandum as amended;

(c) a printed copy of the Articles as amended.

The Registrar will issue a Certificate of Incorporation as a limited company and it is at this point that the change becomes effective and that the changes to the Memorandum and Articles take effect.

■ CHECK LIST ■

PRIVATE COMPANY RE-REGISTERED AS A PUBLIC
 COMPANY

A company may not re-register as a public company
 if previously it has been re-registered as unlimited. ☐

A special resolution is required to alter the Memorandum
 as a public company and to alter other items as necessary. ☐

A special resolution is required to alter the Articles
 as necessary. ☐

The Memorandum and Articles to be printed as altered. ☐

An Auditors' statement on the sufficiency of net
 assets is required. ☐

Is there a relevant balance sheet made up within
 the stipulated time limits? ☐

Is there an unqualified Auditors' Report attached
 to that balance sheet? ☐

Is a valuation report required, is it available and
 was it produced within the stipulated time limits? ☐

Does the company have sufficient issued share capital? ☐

Are there any partly paid shares and do they
 comply with the public company limits? ☐

Are there any shares issued against promises to do
 work or perform services or against undertakings
 and have appropriate arrangements been made? ☐

The company must not start to operate as a public
 company until the Registrar's Certificate is issued. ☐

PUBLIC COMPANY RE-REGISTERED AS A PRIVATE
 COMPANY

A public company may re-register as a company
 limited by shares or by guarantee. ☐

■ CHECK LIST ■

A special resolution is required to alter the
Memorandum and Articles as necessary. ☐

Dissident members may apply to the Court for
the resolution to be set aside. ☐

Are there likely to be sufficient members against the
resolution to meet the minimum number requirements
for an application to be made to the Court? ☐

If an application is made to the Court then the
Registrar must be advised forthwith. ☐

If an application is made to the Court, when a
decision has been reached a copy of the Court
Order must be sent to the Registrar within 15
days of it being made. ☐

Re-registration may only proceed if the special resolution
has been confirmed by the Court or no objection to it
has been raised within the time limits. ☐

The Memorandum or Articles must be printed as
altered. ☐

The company must not start to operate as a private
company until the Registrar's Certificate is issued. ☐

LIMITED COMPANY RE-REGISTERED AS AN UNLIMITED COMPANY

A public company or a company which has previously been
re-registered as a limited company may not re-register
as an unlimited company. ☐

Alterations will be required to the Memorandum
and Articles. ☐

All members must agree to the change. ☐

The Memorandum and Articles must be printed
as altered. ☐

274

■ CHECK LIST ■

The company must not start to operate as an unlimited
company until the Registrar's Certificate is issued. ☐

UNLIMITED COMPANY RE-REGISTERED AS A LIMITED COMPANY

An unlimited company may not re-register as a public
company nor as a limited company if it has been
re-registered as unlimited. ☐

A special resolution is required to alter the
Memorandum and to alter the Memorandum
and Articles if it is to be limited by guarantee. ☐

The Memorandum and Articles are to be printed
as altered. ☐

The company must not start to operate as a limited
company until the Registrar's Certificate is issued. ☐

Striking off and dissolution

■ **CHAPTER TWENTY-TWO** ■

Contents

■ KEY QUESTIONS ■

Is the company surplus to requirements a private company?

Has it ceased trading and does it have any creditors?

Has it engaged in any of the prohibited activities within the past three months?

Have insolvency proceedings been commenced or are they likely to be commenced or has any arrangement been made with creditors?

Have any associated parties any reasons to raise objections?

Does the company have any assets?

Has the application been signed by the requisite number of Directors?

Has the copy of the application been sent to all persons required to be notified?

Has any situation arisen requiring the application to be withdrawn?

Have the Directors complied with all the provisions in connection with the striking-off application?

Have the company records been stored in a safe place should an application for the restoration of the company be made?

22:1 Methods of striking-off

There are three main ways of winding-up a company and removing it from the register of companies at Companies House. These are:

(1) formal winding-up procedure either as a creditors' voluntary winding-up, members' voluntary winding-up or by an order of the court;

(2) at the instigation of the Registrar because he believes that the company is no longer operating; or

(3) at the request of the Directors when the company has ceased trading.

22:1.1 Formal winding-up procedure

If a company is unable to meet its debts and becomes insolvent the case will be handed over to the Official Receiver or to an Insolvency Practitioner who will liquidate the company. This could be as a creditors' voluntary winding-up where the Directors are unable to provide a statutory declaration of solvency or by an order of the court. Where the Directors are able to provide a statutory declaration of solvency the members can resolve to wind-up the company as a members' voluntary liquidation.

The liquidator will collect in the debts of the company, realise the assets and settle the claims of the creditors as far as he/she is able. Should there be surplus assets after the costs of liquidation and all the claims of the creditors have been met those assets will be distributed to the shareholders. The Officers of the company will not be involved with the winding-up of the company other than providing information to the liquidator to enable him/her to wind up the company and make the necessary reports to the Department of Trade and Industry.

22:1.2 Striking-off by the Registrar

If the Registrar is of the opinion that a company is no longer operating he can initiate the striking-off of the company. This would normally take place when returns required from the company have not been filed and/or mail addressed to the company at its registered office is returned undelivered. If enquiries made by the Registrar satisfy him that the company is no longer in business he may place a notice in the *Gazette* that he intends to strike-off the company. Interested parties such as creditors may make representations to the Registrar if they feel the company should not be struck-off.

If after not less than three months after the publication of the notice in the *Gazette* no representations have been received, or those received have been discounted, then the Registrar may dissolve the company by the publication of a further notice in the *Gazette*. Any assets held by the company at the time of dissolution become *bona vacantia* and revert to the Crown.

22:1.3   Striking-off at the Directors' request

The situation can arise where a company is no longer required for the purposes envisaged when it was formed and it is desired to have it struck-off the register at Companies House. The expense of a formal winding-up is not justified and to ignore the continuing obligations of the company in the hope that the Registrar will strike-off the company is a most unsatisfactory way of conducting business affairs. This latter course of action is also most imprudent for the Directors because if they are traced by the Registrar they could lay themselves open to penalties for not maintaining the company's records at Companies House.

There is now, however, under ss.652A – F of the Deregulation and Contracting Out Act 1994 a procedure by which the Directors may make application to the Registrar for a private company to be struck-off. This procedure is described in the following sections of this chapter.

22:2   Application for striking-off

A private company may make an application to be struck off the register when it has ceased to trade and is no longer required and preferably has no creditors. An application may not be made if within the three months prior to the date of the application the company has:

(a)   traded or carried on business in any way;

(b)   changed its name;

(c)   disposed for value any of its trading stock (disposal of capital assets during this period would not prevent an application being made);

(d)   engaged in any activity other than one necessary or conducive to the winding-up of the company.

A company cannot apply to be struck-off if it is the subject, or the proposed subject, of:

(a) any insolvency proceedings, including where a petition has been presented but has not yet been heard; or

(b) a compromise or scheme of arrangement between the company and its creditors or members.

It is also advisable prior to making an application for striking-off to check with any person who could raise an objection and to endeavour to settle his/her concerns before the legal processes are commenced. This would include anyone entitled to receive a copy of the application, listed in **Para. 22:3** below. It would also include local authorities if there were any unresolved matters involving planning permission, the Health and Safety Executive if there were any health and safety issues outstanding, other government agencies which have been involved with the company especially where grants have been made and insurance companies if there are any claims outstanding.

When a company is dissolved under this procedure any assets held by the company become *bona vacantia* and revert to the Crown.

22:3 Submission of the application

The application for striking-off is made on Form 652a which must be signed and dated by:

(a) the sole Director if there is only one Director;

(b) by both Directors if there are only two Directors; or

(c) by a majority of Directors if there are more than two Directors.

The form must also give the name, address and telephone number of a contact should Companies House have any queries about the application. The form, together with a filing fee of £10, must be sent to the Registrar.

Within seven days of submitting the Form 652a to Companies House the company must provide copies to all of the following persons:

(a) the members;

(b) the creditors (This would include both existing and prospective creditors, normal trade creditors, former employees if they are owed money, guarantors and personal injury claimants. Further the government tax collecting departments must be advised if there are any outstanding, contingent or prospective liabilities.);

(c) any employees;

(d) managers or trustees of any employee pension fund;

(e) any Directors who did not sign the form.

Any person who becomes a member or creditor after the application for striking-off has been made must be sent a copy of Form 652a within seven days of acquiring the interest. If a company is still registered for VAT at the time the application is made the relevant VAT office must also be informed.

The copies of the form must be delivered or posted to the last known address of an individual or to the registered or principal office in the case of a company or a partnership. If the company has had dealings with more than one office of an organisation then a copy of the form should be sent to each establishment with which the company has had dealings.

22:4 Registration of application at Companies House

If the Registrar is satisfied that the application has been correctly made he will place it on the company's file at Companies House. The Registrar will send an acknowledgement of receipt to the address shown on the application and also to the company's registered office. The Registrar will also place a notice in the *Gazette* that an application to strike-off the company has been received.

Once the application is placed on the company's file it is in the public domain and it is open to any interested party to object to the striking-off of the company. Objections must be in writing and sent to the Registrar together with any supporting evidence to support the objection. Reasons why an objection to the striking-off may be lodged with the Registrar would include:

(a) if any of the conditions precedent to an application being submitted have been broken;

(b) that the Directors have not informed interested parties;

(c) if any of the declarations made on the application are false;

(d) should some action be currently taken, or be pending, to recover money from the company;

(e) any other legal action being taken against the company;

(f) that the Directors have been engaged in wrongful trading, have committed a tax fraud or committed some other offence.

22:5 Withdrawal of application

The Directors must withdraw their application for striking-off if the company ceases to be eligible under these regulations. The withdrawal is effected by submission to Companies House of Form 652c signed by any Director. The filing fee of £10 submitted with Form 652a is not refundable upon the application being withdrawn.

The application for striking-off must be withdrawn if any of the activities listed below take place:

(a) the company trades or otherwise carries on business;

(b) the company disposes of any property or rights for value other than any held to facilitate the process of its application;

(c) the company becomes the subject of formal insolvency proceedings or makes a compromise or arrangement with its creditors;

(d) the company engages in any other activity other than one necessary or conducive to making an application for striking-off.

22:6 The dissolution of the company

If after not less than three months after the Registrar published the notice in the *Gazette* he knows of no reason why the company should not be dissolved and the application has not been withdrawn then he will proceed with the striking-off. The company is officially dissolved when the Registrar publishes a further notice in the *Gazette* to that effect. The Registrar will also advise the contact person named on the original application of the proposed date of dissolution.

22:7 Offences under these provisions

Failure to comply with the regulations for any of the reasons set out below is an offence which could attract penalties upon the Directors in default. Failure:

(a) to make an application for striking-off when the company is ineligible;

(b) to provide false or misleading information in an application or in support of an application;

(c) to send a copy of the application within seven days of it being made to all interested parties;

(d) to withdraw the application if the company becomes ineligible.

A person in default can be liable to a fine of up to £5,000 in a court of summary jurisdiction and an unlimited fine on indictment. Directors, if found guilty of deliberately concealing from interested parties that an application has been made, may be liable for up to seven years imprisonment in addition to any fines that may be imposed. These offences could also be a cause for the disqualification of a Director from holding office in a company or being in any way concerned in the management of a company.

22:8 Restoration of a company to the register

When a company has been struck-off it is open for interested parties to make an application to the court for the company to be restored to the register. Probably the most common causes for applications for restoration are when a further creditor of the company comes to light, further assets of the company are discovered or a person wishes to make a claim against the company, especially for industrial injury, such claims if successful being met by the company's former insurers.

In England and Wales application would be made to the High Court or to a District Registry or to a County Court which has authority to wind-up a company; in Scotland application would be made to the Court of Session or if the paid-up capital does not exceed £120,000 it may be made to the Sheriff Court in the sheriffdom in which the registered office of the company was situated. Application for restoration can be made in the following circumstances and is dependent on the manner in which the company was struck-off.

22:8.1 Struck-off following a Form 652a application

An application for a company to be restored to the register following a Form 652a application may be made by any person who was entitled to be given a copy of the original application and must be made within 20 years of the date of dissolution. The court may order the restoration if it is satisfied that:

(a) the person was entitled to a copy of the application but was not so supplied;

(b) the application was in breach of the conditions appertaining thereto;

(c) there are other reasons for which the court considers it is just so to do.

The Secretary of State for Trade and Industry may also apply to the court for the restoration of a company to the register if he feels it is justified in the public interest.

22:8.2 Struck-off at the instigation of the Registrar

When a company has been struck-off at the instigation of the Registrar the company, a member or a creditor may apply for its restoration to the register. If the application is made by the company it must be joined by a member to give the necessary undertakings to the court. The application must be made within 20 years of the dissolution of the company.

22:8.3 Dissolved by formal liquidation proceedings

Where a company has been dissolved following formal liquidation proceedings the liquidator or any other interested party (e.g. a creditor) may make application for the company to be restored to the register. Normally such an application must be made within two years of the winding-up of the company. An application can, however, be made at any time where the purpose is to bring proceedings against a company for:

(a)   damages for personal injuries; or

(b)   damages under the Fatal Accidents Act 1976 or the Damages (Scotland) Act 1976.

22:9   Procedure for restoration

In England and Wales a copy of the application to the court must be served on the solicitor dealing with any *bona vacantia* assets which would be the Treasury Solicitor or the Solicitor to the Duchy of Cornwall or the Duchy of Lancaster (if appropriate) and on the Registrar at Companies House. In Scotland it should served on the Lord Advocate, the Queen's and Lord Treasurer's Remembrancer (Q & LTR) who supervises *bona vacantia* assets and on the Registrar.

The court will require an affidavit or witness statement that:

(a)   the originating document was served; and

(b)   the solicitor dealing with any *bona vacantia* assets has no objection.

The statement should also cover the following matters, as appropriate:

(a)   when the company was incorporated and its objects, accompanied by a copy of the Certificate of Incorporation, the Memorandum and the Articles;

(b)   its membership and its officers;

(c)   its trading activity and when it stopped trading;

(d)   an explanation of any failure to deliver any documents to the Registrar;

(e)   details of the striking-off and dissolution of the company;

(f)   the company's solvency;

(g)   any other supporting information to this application for restoration.

Prior to the court hearing, the Registrar will require any statutory documents necessary to bring up to date the company's file at Companies House to be delivered to him, and for any irregularities in the company's corporate structure to be resolved. Any costs of the Treasury Solicitor, the Lord Advocate or other person who represents the Registrar must be met by the applicant and any late filing penalties incurred in bringing up to date the filing of annual accounts must be met by the company.

An office copy of the court order bearing the court's seal must be delivered to the Registrar by the applicant and the company is regarded as restored to the register when it has been so delivered.

■ CHECK LIST ■

Is the company that is going to be struck-off private, has it ceased trading and has it satisfied all of its creditors? ☐

Have any of the prohibited activities taken place within the last three months? ☐

Have any insolvency proceedings been commenced against the company or any notice of proceedings been served on the company? ☐

Has any arrangement been made with the creditors of the company? ☐

Have all other past associates and official bodies with whom the company has had dealings confirmed that they have no latent claims against the company? ☐

Does the company have any assets which would revert to the Crown? ☐

Has the application been signed by the requisite number of Directors? ☐

Has everyone entitled to receive a copy of the application been so supplied? ☐

Has anyone become entitled to a copy of the application since it was first made and have they been so supplied? ☐

Has acknowledgement of receipt of the application been received from Companies House? ☐

Have any objections to striking-off been received? ☐

Has the company become ineligible for striking-off and if so has Form 652c been submitted? ☐

Have all of the regulations been observed by the Directors? ☐

■ CHECK LIST ■

Has notice of the dissolution of the company been
posted in the *Gazette*? ☐

Have all of the statutory books and other company
records been stored in a safe place? ☐

Has an application for restoration of the
company to the register been made? ☐

Have all the filing requirements been brought
up to date? ☐

Glossary

Accounting Reference Date:

The date of the company's own choosing to which the accounts for the year must be prepared.

Annual General Meeting:

The general meeting of members which each company must hold each year and not more than 15 months after the previous year's meeting. A private company may now pass an elective resolution to dispense with holding an Annual General Meeting.

Annual Return:

Form 363 which must be returned each year to Companies House. Now issued individually to every company registered with information from Companies House records to be confirmed or amended as necessary.

Articles of Association:

The rule book of the company. A company limited by shares need not register Articles upon incorporation as Table A of the Act, under which the company was registered, will apply unless specifically excluded.

Bonus issue:

An issue of shares made to members in proportion to their existing holdings, the shares having been paid-up by the capitalisation of profits otherwise available for distribution as dividends.

Charges:

Charges are given by a company to a third party as security for money lent to, or owed by, the company. Should the company become insolvent or otherwise unable to meet its obligations the third party may realise the assets charged to recover the money owed, in preference to other creditors.

Fixed charge – where the security is a specific asset.

Floating charge – where the security is the whole undertaking of the company.

Common seal:

A mechanical device for impressing the company's name upon documents which when attested in accordance with the Articles enables a company to execute a deed.

Cum-dividend:

An expression used when shares are transferred and the entitlement to a dividend already declared but not yet paid passes to the purchaser.

Directors:

Alternate – A person who acts only when his/her principal is absent. The alternate must be registered at Companies House as a Director.

Executive – A Director who works as a full time employee of the company.

Non-executive – A Director who works part-time for the company or who has no involvement with the company other than attending board meetings.

Shadow – A person who has not been appointed a Director but in accordance with whose advice or instructions the board are accustomed to act.

Debenture:

A charge created by the company. It may be fixed or floating and issued as a single document or as a series of documents.

Dormant company:

One which has no financial transactions within its financial year to pass through its books of account, though a newly incorporated company whose only transactions are the receipt of monies in respect of the issue of shares in accordance with the Memorandum will be regarded as dormant. A dormant company must still file an Annual Report and Accounts and an Annual Return each year.

Extraordinary General Meeting:

Any general meeting of members other than the Annual General Meeting. Usually called by the Directors but may be demanded by the members.

Ex-dividend:

An expression used when shares are transferred and the entitlement to a dividend which has been declared but not yet paid does not pass to the purchaser but remains with the vendor.

Members of a company:

The members are the holders of shares in the company of all classes. Debenture holders are not members but creditors with special rights. The first members are the persons subscribing to the Memorandum. In the case of a guarantee company without a share capital the members are those persons undertaking to contribute to the assets of the company should it become insolvent.

Memorandum:
The constitution of the company which must be filed with the Registrar upon incorporation.

Officer of the company:
Defined by s.744 as a Director, Manager or Secretary of the company.

Options:
Options or rights are granted by a company when the holder may at some future date subscribe for shares from the company at a price fixed or ascertainable from a quoted formula at the time that the option is granted.

Pre-emption rights:
The rights which a shareholder has upon a further issue of shares by the company to insist that he/she be allowed to subscribe for the same proportion of the new issue that his/her existing holding bears to the total shares currently in issue.

Poll:
A vote taken at a general meeting of members where each member has one vote for every share held or in some other proportion as laid down in the Articles.

Proxy:
A person who is appointed by a member to attend and vote in his/her place at a general meeting of members.

Quorum:
The minimum number of persons who must be present at a meeting for that meeting to be validly constituted.

The Registrar:
The titular head of Companies House in whose name actions by that organisation are undertaken. In some large companies it is also the title given to a person charged with the responsibility for maintaining the company's Register of Members.

Resolutions:
Special – Passed by a 75 per cent majority at a meeting of which 21 days' notice has been given.

Extraordinary – Passed by a 75 per cent majority at a meeting of which 14 days' notice has been given.

Ordinary – Passed by a majority of 50 per cent at a meeting of which 14 days' notice has been given.

Elective – Approved by everyone entitled to attend and vote at a meeting of which 21 days' notice has been given.

Scrip issue:
An alternative term for a bonus issue.

Secretary of State:
The titular head of the Department of Trade and Industry (DTI) in whose name the actions of that organisation are undertaken.

Shares:
The portions into which the capital of a company is divided. The rights of the holders of any particular shares are as set out in that company's Articles, though the conditions mentioned below are commonplace.

Ordinary – Have unrestricted rights to dividends and to share in any surplus on a winding-up. Also have voting rights in proportion to the size of holding.

Preference – Entitled to a fixed maximum dividend in preference to the ordinary shares but to no further participation in the profits. On a winding-up entitled to repayment in preference to the ordinary shares but to no further participation in any surplus. Have voting rights only in certain limited circumstances.

Share certificates:
Certificates of title to shares in a company.

Stock:
The division of the capital of the company into units expressed in monetary terms, usually multiples of 100. Also used in defining company loan stocks and debentures and government securities issued to the public.

Table A:
The model set of Articles included in the Companies Acts.

Transfer of shares:
The document used to transfer ownership of shares or stock and, when stamped by the Inland Revenue or certified as not liable to stamp duty, is the instruction to the company to amend their Register of Members and to issue a share certificate to the purchaser.

Transmission of shares:
  The passage of shares registered in the name of a deceased person in accordance with their will or the instructions of their executor or administrator.

Ultra Vires:
  An action by the Directors, or by the company for which they are responsible, which is outside the powers given in the Objects Clause in the Memorandum.

Wrongful trading:
  The failure of a Director or a Shadow Director of a company which has gone into insolvent liquidation to cease trading when that person knew or should have known that there was no reasonable prospect of avoiding insolvency.

Index

This index is in alphabetical, word by word order. It does not cover the contents list, introduction, key questions, check lists or glossary. Location references in the index refer to paragraph number. There is no reference to page numbers.

For example:

indicates that information on the retention of accounting records can be found in Chapter 3, Secretarial aspects of annual accounts, under the heading **3**:1.4, Retention of records.

Abbreviations: App = Appendix